The Contemporary Challenge of
Modernist Theology

The Contemporary Challenge of Modernist Theology

Paul Badham

UNIVERSITY OF WALES PRESS
CARDIFF
1998

© Paul Badham, 1998

British Library Cataloguing-in-Publication Data.
A catalogue record for this book is available from the British Library.

ISBN 0–7083–1501–1 (cased)
    0–7083–1503–8 (paperback)

Typeset by Action Publishing Technology, Gloucester
Printed in Great Britain by Gwasg Dinefwr, Llandybïe

Contents

Preface

This book is written to celebrate the centenary of what is now known as the Modern Churchpeople's Union (MCU). This is a dynamic, lively society of liberal-minded Christians which publishes a flourishing journal called *Modern Believing* and every year holds a significant and well-attended conference on a theme of importance to contemporary Christianity.

In this context it may seem surprising that throughout this book I have focused on Modernists who did their main work before the Second World War and I have often spoken of Modernism in the past tense. The reason for this is that the Modernists used to be a clearly defined party with a very specific theological agenda. Their early conferences were attended by a close-knit group, most of whom were Anglican clergy who either held academic posts or at any rate devoted large parts of their lives to theological study. The same people usually read papers at the conferences year after year and, as Alan Stephenson has shown, one can give a convincing sketch of what a typical Modernist believed.[1] R. J. Page, in his history of Anglican theology, says: 'English Modernism prepared the way for radicalism but declined in influence as increasingly it came to be seen as a recognizable body of theological conclusions.'[2] The reason for the decline, however, was not the existence of a readily recognizable Modernist position but, rather, that this position came to be thought of as outmoded. Consequently Modernism was displaced initially by a widespread return to more traditional viewpoints, and then in the 1960s and 1980s by the ideas of more radical thinkers who were willing to jettison far more of historic Christianity than their Modernist predecessors.

What has really surprised me, and I hope will interest the reader, is how much the tide of opinion has recently swung round in favour of the classic Modernist position. One pointer in this direction may be that membership of the MCU and circulation of its journal have both increased dramatically recently and its centenary conference was fully booked weeks in advance. But more significant is the fact that intellectual discussion of religious issues has shown a burgeoning interest in precisely those areas of religious belief which were of greatest concern to the classic Modernist. In particular I have highlighted in this book a resurgence of interest in the relationship between religion, philosophy and science, a new interest in the historical Jesus and in how he reveals God to us, a new spirit of questioning into the meaning and significance of his resurrection and in beliefs in life after death and a new openness to religious experiencing and to the beliefs of people of other faiths.

All these issues are of deep concern to contemporary members of the MCU, though unlike the situation in the past there is no required Modernist line today. The MCU now embraces a wide spectrum of liberal and radical thought, and its conferences and its journal are no longer dominated by insiders but offer their hospitality to a range of interesting speakers and authors who wish to help Christianity to face the challenge of the new millennium. In this context it is interesting to see how much the Modernist heritage has to contribute to the present debate, and how many of the liveliest issues of today are precisely those that were addressed by earlier members of this vibrant society.

Paul Badham
January 1998

1

What is Modernism?

The word 'Modernism' in relation to theology in Britain is historically identified with the position championed by the Modern Church People's Union (MCU), a pressure group within and beyond the Anglican Church which was founded in 1898 and therefore celebrated its centenary in 1998. Modernism was especially influential in the 1920s and 1930s, when a significant proportion of leading Christian thinkers belonged to this Union, and a plethora of articulate defences of Christianity were published which were proud to include the word 'Modernist' within their titles.[1] The movement is generally held to have reached the peak of its influence with the publication of the report of the Archbishops' Commission on *Doctrine in the Church of England*[2] in 1938 which either endorsed or recognized as permissible certain liberal reinterpretations of Christian beliefs. Since then the movement as such has gone into decline, though I hope to show that what the Modernists saw as the heart of the Gospel corresponds to the issues being debated by those interested in religious themes at the start of the new millennium more closely than any of the schools of thought that have been influential in the intervening years.

'English Modernism', as it is generally called to distinguish it from Roman Catholic Modernism,[3] grew out of the 'Broad Church' movement of the nineteenth century and shared its concern about the implications for traditional understandings of Christianity of taking seriously 'modern thought'. By this was meant accepting the legitimacy of such nineteenth-century developments as the rise of historical criticism, the spread of Utilitarian ethical theory and the widespread acceptance of the theory of evolution. What Broad Churchmen, Liberal Protestants and Modernists all recognized was that, in the light of the new learning, the way Christianity was articulated and expressed had to be modified if it was to continue to speak to the contemporary world. In essence, the Broad Church thinkers of the nineteenth century identified the challenges that the new learning brought to many areas of traditional belief, and the Liberal Protestants focused on the way a new approach to the Bible should affect the way Christians understood the Gospels, and in particular the interpretation of the person and work of Jesus Christ. The English Modernists drew on both these traditions, but also took over further insights and the name 'Modernists' from the Catholic Modernists, who were condemned by Pope Pius X in 1907.[4] What the Catholic Modernists contributed was a sense that living Christianity cannot simply be identified with the rediscovery of its original message as if centuries of Christian experience and development had contributed nothing to the faith. Likewise Christianity is not simply a matter of individual believing, for Christianity has a communal dimension in the life of the Church. Hence many of the English Modernists had a strong interest in Church history and in the development of doctrine over the centuries. They also believed it to be important that the Church as a whole should come to terms with the new knowledge. Hence the English Modernists were not content simply to urge the right of individual scholars to reinterpret for themselves the meaning of Christianity. They also sought to persuade the Anglican Church to accept the need for a new approach to the Gospel, and hence it was extremely important to them that the Doctrine Commission of 1938 should recognize the legitimacy of Modernist theology as one way of interpreting the Christian message.

The essential characteristic of Modernism is the belief that Christian faith needs to be restated in the light of modern knowledge. This restatement would require the rejection of beliefs which on historical or scientific grounds are no longer tenable. However, Modernists believe that a kernel of truth can be separated from the surrounding husk of outmoded thought without losing the heart of the original belief. For example, it is characteristic of classic Modernism that any authentic belief in divine creation today requires disbelief in the literal truth of Genesis and a full acceptance of the theory of evolution. Similarly, Modernists have argued that belief in biblical inspiration must be wholly separated from belief in biblical infallibility and must recognize the validity of the historical–critical methodology of modern scholarship. It is characteristic of Modernism to wish to affirm the divinity of Christ while treating as legendary the story of the Virgin Birth and while refusing to be bound to the philosophical categories of the Chalcedonian Definition. Belief in the resurrection of Jesus Christ does not necessarily require the physical emptiness of his tomb, any more than belief in life after death in general requires belief in the literal resurrection of our ashes after cremation.

However, Modernism has always regarded itself as an essentially positive movement. The purpose is not to deny but to affirm the truths that matter. Let me quote three testimonies from H. D. A. Major's classic work *English Modernism*. First George Tyrell: 'By a Modernist I mean a churchman of any sort who believes in the possibility of a synthesis between the essential truth of his religion and the essential truth of modernity.' Second, Percy Gardner: 'Modernism is based upon evolution in science and the critical method in history; and it demands, not that the great truths of the Christian religion shall be given up, but that they shall be considered afresh in the light of growing knowledge, and restated in a way suitable to the intellectual conditions of the age.' Third, Dr Sanday: 'I aim at thinking the thoughts and speaking the language of my own day, and yet, at the same time, keeping all that is essential in the religion of the past.'[5]

From the perspective of the new millennium, the positive aspect of Modernism can much better be appreciated now than in earlier years. Compared with the radical theologians of the 1960s and 1970s or with the Sea of Faith movement of the 1980s, Modernism is deeply committed to the central beliefs of historic Christianity. In his Hulsean Lectures tracing the history of the English Modernists from 1898 to 1984, Alan Stephenson gives a 'thumbnail sketch of the beliefs of the typical English Modernist'. His sketch covers the core Modernist beliefs, though, as we shall see, it needs expansion. I cite below the key features of his description, apologizing only that as late as the 1980s even Modernists still used gender-exclusive language!

The typical Modernist

was totally convinced of the existence of God . . . but a God who worked only through the evolutionary process . . . He believed in a God who could be known, to a certain extent in other religions, but who was supremely revealed in the Logos. He had no doubt about the existence of Jesus Christ ... His Christology was a degree Christology ... His Jesus was not an eschatological figure but rather the Lord of Thought who proclaimed the Fatherhood of God and the Brotherhood of Man. His doctrine of the atonement was Abelardian or exemplarist. He had no hesitation in accepting all that biblical criticism had to say, as far as it had advanced by the death of B. H. Streeter in 1937. He maintained that he believed in the supernatural but not in the miraculous. His Jesus therefore did not perform miracles. He was not born of a virgin and his resurrection was a spiritual one ... He had a strong belief in the life after death and was a universalist ... For the most part he was a Liberal Protestant ... He believed in the reform and revision of the 1662 Book of Common Prayer. He was an advocate of the ordination of women and of the marriage of the divorced in church. On sexual matters he was ahead of his contemporaries, advocating contraception when many churchmen were still rigorously opposed to it ... He did not believe in a this-worldly Utopia. His vision was clearly set on the life of the world to come.[6]

Stephenson's summary is based on his reading of the whole corpus of Modernist writings, from the works of its leading authors to the articles published in the *Modern Churchman*, and the papers given at their conferences. What I would wish to highlight from this list of beliefs is the Modernists' absolute conviction of the reality of God and of a life after death. They saw these beliefs as the corner-stone of Christianity without which faith would be empty of any significance or meaning. The Modernists believed that theism could be rationally defended by philosophical argument and was fully compatible with a scientific understanding of the nature of reality. They also urged that Christian mysticism or religious experience must be added to those factors reckoned as foundational for Christian faith. As a revealed religion, Christianity depends not only on the authority of the Bible or the Church but also on the individual's consciousness of God. This was particularly stressed by Dean W. R. Inge, who argued:

At the present time, our greatest need seems to me that we should return to the fundamentals of spiritual religion. We

cannot shut our eyes to the fact that both the old seats of authority, the infallible Church and the infallible book, are fiercely
assailed, and that our faith needs reinforcements. These can only
come from the depths of the religious consciousness itself, and if
summoned from thence they will not be found wanting. The
'impregnable rock' is neither an institution nor a book, but a life
or experience.[7]

This stress on experience was one reason why Modernists were
confident that God could be known through other world faiths.
They were confident that the Logos made known through Christ
was also at work in other religious traditions. Hence, from the
beginning Modernists were sympathetic to the study of comparative religion; indeed, William Boyd Carpenter, who as Bishop of
Ripon founded the theological college most associated with
Modernism, believed that the study of other religions must be
part of 'the education of a minister of God'.[8]

One element in Stephenson's summary of Modernist beliefs
which needs expansion is the importance Modernists attached to
faith in Jesus Christ as God incarnate. Stephenson shows elsewhere in his book that he is fully aware of this, and cites Hastings
Rashdall's claim that belief in 'a unique and paramount revelation of God in the historic Christ' needs to be set alongside 'belief
in a personal God and a personal immortality', these together
forming 'the three great essentials of the Christian religion'.
Rashdall argued that these three beliefs set the limits on 'Clerical
Liberalism' and he uncompromisingly affirmed:

> I would not wish the ministry of the Church of England made
> accessible to persons who do not believe in Theism and human
> immortality, and who do not recognise the unique and para-
> mount character of the Christian revelation in a sense which
> makes it possible for them, without a feeling of unreality, to use
> the ordinary language of the Church about the Divinity of our
> Lord.[9]

Henry Major, the 'arch-apostle' of Modernism, is even stronger.
According to him, 'English Modernism is essentially Christo-
centric.' Indeed it 'may be charged with Jesuolatry because it
adores the Godhead as unveiled in the personality, teaching and
spirit of Jesus'.[10] In some ways what Major says is reminiscent of

the claim made by Friedrich Schleiermacher, that Christianity is 'essentially distinguished' from other monotheistic faiths by the way in which 'everything is related to the redemption accomplished by Jesus of Nazareth'.[11] For the 'father of modern theology', just as much as for Major, coming to terms with belief in the deity of Christ is as important as belief in God and immortality – 'those first articles of any religious belief'.[12]

As we shall see, the importance of Christology to the classical Modernists was often obscured in the debates of the 1920s by their opponents, who believed that only Chalcedonian orthodoxy and total adherence to such beliefs as the Virgin Birth or the bodily resurrection of Jesus could safeguard Christ's divinity. But the Modernists themselves had no doubt of their total commitment. It was precisely because of this commitment to Christ that they believed that the traditional doctrine had to be re-expressed in modern terms in order that it might continue to be believed.

Concerning the historical Jesus, most Modernists were highly optimistic that a great deal could be known about Jesus by the appropriate use of modern historiography. Stephenson is thus wholly right to suggest that Modernists in general accepted the findings of New Testament scholarship up to that of B. H. Streeter, who died in 1937, but did not go along with the more radical scepticism of Rudolf Bultmann, whose work appeared from the 1930s. This fact is obscured by the controversy associated with Bishop E. W. Barnes's book *The Rise of Christianity* published in 1947. This book took a very negative view of the historical origins of Christianity and was frequently described as representative of the Modernist position, even though it was trenchantly reviewed in the *Modern Churchman,* and both the MCU Council and leading Modernist scholars such as Inge distanced themselves from the work as a book likely to do grave harm to the Modernist cause by its atypical scepticism.[13] In fact most MCU members presupposed that the Liberal Protestant position of Adolf von Harnack's *What is Christianity?* remained valid, and those who went further than Harnack accepted the conclusions of Streeter on the Gospel sources but did not accept the views of R. H. Lightfoot or Bultmann, that we can know little of the historical Jesus. Typical Modernists were very confident in the essential historicity of Jesus' life and teaching, while reserving judgement on the miracle stories.

One very striking feature of Stephenson's history of the Modernist movement is that it reads like an obituary. He suggests possible dates when Modernism 'died', and the assumption throughout his work is that he is chronicling a movement with a great past but no future. Stephenson takes for granted that no contemporary thinker will be a Modernist: 'The theology of the great Modernists of the past has been superseded and no longer has its protagonists.'[14] In 1984 this was an understandable position: for traditional Christians the influence of Karl Barth's Neo-orthodoxy and its British parallel, the Biblical Theology movement, had led many to believe that the broad framework of traditional belief could be proclaimed without heeding the Modernist critique. On the other side, Liberal Christians from the 1960s onwards explored a variety of theologies which were all far more critical of the Christian heritage than was that of the classic Modernists. Under the influence of John Robinson's *Honest to God,* a great interest developed in Bultmann's call for the demythologization of the Christian message, in Paul Tillich's quest for a post-theistic ultimate concern and in Dietrich Bonhoeffer's talk of a 'Religionless Christianity'. Subsequent thinkers looked for the secular meaning of the Gospel,[15] spoke of the 'Death of God'[16] and finally, with Don Cupitt, argued that if religious values were in any way to be preserved we must jettison belief in an objective God or afterlife and recognize that all our beliefs are simply constructs of human language.[17] Hence, neither defenders nor critics of mainstream Christianity had a serious interest in the Modernist vision of a central core of belief being liberated from connection with outmoded dogmas.

Now, however, the wheel has turned full circle, in that the issues that concerned the Modernists appear once more to have come to the forefront of contemporary religious debate. These issues can be listed as follows:

1. Belief that the objective existence of God can be shown to be compatible with modern philosophy and science.
2. Belief that religious experience is foundational for faith and that such experience is part of the common heritage of the world's faiths.
3. Belief in the reality of life after death understood in terms of the immortality of the soul.

4. Belief that the divinity of Christ must be expressed in such a way that it is compatible with the equally important doctrine of his humanity and oneness with us and that it genuinely reflects what historical study of the Gospels tells us about Jesus' life and thought.

To suggest that such issues really are of great contemporary interest will strike many Churchpeople as surprising. This is because, regrettably, today much of this debate is not happening in ecclesiastical circles, and, indeed, many Church leaders do not seem to see the importance of such discussion. Yet belief in God, Christ, spirituality and life after death are all crucial to any form of living Christianity. Thus, it would seem important for more Churchpeople to know that a lively discussion about God is taking place among many contemporary philosophers and scientists, that religious experience or 'spirituality' is an increasingly popular quest among young people, that the historical figure of Jesus continues to fascinate both historians and the general public, and that there has been an explosion of interest in the possibility of life after death in the light of claims following 'near-death experiences'. I have entitled this book *The Contemporary Challenge of Modernist Theology* to highlight the fact that the themes that the Modernists addressed in the 1920s and 1930s really are crucial to living faith and need to be addressed within the Churches as well as in the communities of scholarship and general interest.

Consider the question of the existence of God. Throughout the nineteenth century and for most of the twentieth it was axiomatic in a number of intellectual circles that the fading-away of belief in God would be an inevitable consequence of the spread of scientific and rational thought. As early as 1882, Friedrich Nietzsche could claim: 'God is dead in the hearts of men, science and rationalism have killed him.'[18] Of course, Nietzsche subsequently recognized that he had been premature: 'I come too early . . . this tremendous event is still on its way.'[19] Yet Nietzsche and many other leading intellectuals of the nineteenth and the early twentieth century, such as Karl Marx or Sigmund Freud or Bertrand Russell, had no doubt that belief in God would die out as scientific knowledge spread. We have already noted that such a view found several champions within the Christian churches in the 'Death of God' movement of the 1960s and the 'Sea of Faith' movement of the 1980s.[20]

However, belief in God has not died out and appears to have undergone, in some quarters at least, a substantial revival. Indeed, according to Paul Johnson, author both of the *History of Christianity* and of *Modern Times,* 'The most extraordinary thing about the twentieth century has been the failure of God to die . . . At the end of the twentieth century, the idea of . . . God is as lively and real as ever.' Johnson believes that the reason for this is that science and religion have come to a new harmony. He even claims that the situation has changed so drastically that the great majority of those who work in the scientific world – perhaps as many as 80 per cent – now profess some kind of religious belief.[21]

In terms of scientists in general, Johnson's figures are obviously wrong, but presumably he must be referring only to scientists working in the area of the so-called 'new physics', where, according to Terry Miethe, 'the argument from design has very recently gained acceptance among many scientists'.[22] Keith Ward makes a similar point about the new physics when he observes in his book *The Turn of the Tide:* 'Just when philosophers had thought that the argument from design was gone for ever, the physicist brings it back again.'[23]

The reason for this, according to Russell Stannard, professor of Physics at the Open University, is that 'the very latest revelations of science, instead of posing fresh difficulties, have led to new harmony, and the methods of investigation used in science and religion, far from being opposed to each other in their outlook, are in many ways similar'.[24] Paul Davies goes even further and insists that, in the light of the new physics, we can legitimately claim that 'science offers a surer path to God than religion'.[25]

Before this sea-change took place among scientists, many, perhaps most, philosophers of religion believed that the arguments for God's existence had been definitively answered by David Hume and Immanuel Kant and that there was little mileage in refuting them except as an introductory exercise for first-year Philosophy students. For example, Kai Nielsen, a Canadian philosopher and a convinced atheist, wrote in 1971 that philosophers who took the claims of religion seriously were 'very much in the minority and their arguments have been forcefully contested'. But nearly twenty years later Nielsen's estimate of philosophical attitudes had changed:

> Philosophy of religion in Anglo-American context has taken a curious turn in the past decade ... what has come to the forefront ... is a group of Christian philosophers of a philosophically analytic persuasion, but hostile to even the residues of logical empiricism or Wittgensteinianism, who return to the old topics and the old theses of traditional Christian philosophy and natural theology.[26]

We should, of course, notice that Nielsen describes this development as 'curious', an indication that he himself is unconvinced by it. We should also note that philosophers not engaged in the current discussions in the philosophy of religion often remain unaffected by it. Nevertheless, if we are looking simply at the current status of the arguments for the existence of God it is interesting to notice Richard Purtill's evaluation of the scene: 'All the traditional arguments have able and respected defenders and if there is not a consensus in favour of philosophical arguments for God's existence it is no longer true that there is a consensus against.'[27]

When we move on to the issue of religious experience, there would probably be a strong consensus in favour of recognizing its importance. Basil Mitchell and Richard Swinburne have argued that it is possible to provide some kind of justification for religious belief and to make out a case for the coherence of theism. But the best one can hope for from such arguments is that they show belief in God to be rational in the sense of its being one possible way of making sense of the way the world is.[28] For the believer, it is the additional personal knowledge which comes from religious experience that tips the balance of probability in favour of real belief. John Hick developed this argument in his essay 'Rational theistic belief without proofs', in which he pointed out that the biblical tradition offers no arguments for God's existence but presents us with people whose

> awareness of God was so vivid that ... they could no more help believing in the reality of God than in the reality of the material world and of their human neighbours ... God was known to the prophets and apostles as a dynamic will interacting with their own wills; a sheerly given personal reality.

Hick correctly argues that for such persons belief in God was as rational as believing in the reality of the perceptual world, for both were experienced as equally given and compelling.[29]

Few today would claim the same overwhelming sense of the presence of God as did the biblical prophets, but many claim at least enough religious awareness to understand the force of this argument. Hence it is common to appeal to personal religious experience as grounds for continuing with the life of faith. Moreover, because the hymns and psalms most popular in worship frequently describe intense religious feelings, uttering such words can often evoke in the worshipper similar feelings to those which initially gave birth to that hymn or psalm. For example to sing 'My God how wonderful thou art' can help to generate the feeling that God is indeed wonderful. So religious feelings can be transmitted across generations. Through singing the songs of one's predecessors in the faith one is enabled to recapitulate and make their experiences one's own. The word 'tradition' etymologically means 'handing on' and it is the case that to share in a heritage of faith can enable experiences central to faith to be handed on and to be made new in each succeeding generation. To accept the centrality of religious experience and to recognize the way in which religious traditions pass on such experiences inevitably opens one to the view that if people in other religious traditions also share in profound religious experience which influence their believing, then we seem logically bound to accept their faith too. Inter-faith relations is an issue which inevitably follows from accepting the importance of religious experience. But we need not labour the importance of inter-faith relations as a theme of contemporary theology since even those most opposed to any dialogue between the world religions affirm this to be 'the issue of the decade'.[30]

To claim that life after death is a major issue of modern religious discussion is not true if we confine our attention to the Christian Churches. The doctrine is not included in the framework of the *Alpha* course of instruction in Christianity originally pioneered by Holy Trinity, Brompton, but now used throughout Britain by all the major denominations as a way of teaching the faith. Similarly it is hard to find reference to life after death in modern hymn-books. According to an article in the journal *Theology*, it is a 'fringe belief' in our society.[31] Likewise, my suggestion that it is discussed today in terms of the 'immortality of the soul' is seriously at odds with contemporary Christian theology, where it has become normal to repudiate the concept of the soul and to insist that the language of resurrection is the only appropriate terminology in which to discuss the Christian hope.

Outside normal theological circles, however, the phenomenon of near-death experiences (NDEs) has revolutionized the situation. Tens of thousands of people have recently been resuscitated from apparent death having had a series of experiences which have usually convinced them of their own immortality. According to the findings of sociologist Allan Kellehear, 'most clinical near-death experiencers are convinced that their experiences are a glimpse of life after death'. Kellehear believes that one of the most important features of the NDE in society has been that 'it put the idea of personal survival of death back on the religious agenda'.[32] This is certainly true of my own experience of teaching courses in Death and Immortality and Philosophy of Religion and in participating in television documentaries on near-death experiences. It is particularly true of so-called New Age religion. Tony Walter, director of the MA course in Death and Society at Reading University, challenges:

> Go to any Christian bookshop in Britain and you will find precious little on life after death. Go to any New Age bookshop and you will find lots ... With the failure of modern Christianity to speak plausibly of a future life, New Agers are taking up the baton that the Christians have fumbled with and dropped.[33]

This is baffling in that historic Christianity more than any other religion has been committed to belief in life after death and it is hard to see how any living faith can exclude this dimension. The Modernists believed passionately in the future hope, and this would seem an area where their insights are most needed by the contemporary Churches.

The fourth claim made in this chapter is that Christology is one of the liveliest issues in contemporary theology and that a new quest for the historical Jesus is a major concern of New Testament scholarship. Here I do not need to justify my claim. No one at all acquainted with recent theological debate or ecclesiastical controversy can doubt that the doctrine of the Person of

Christ is being vigorously discussed in modern theology. Similarly, there is little doubt that historians both theological and general continue to be fascinated by the historical figure of Jesus. How far either of these developments in their contemporary form can be shown to be akin to the debates about the 'Christ of Faith' and the 'Jesus of History' in classic Modernism must await discussion in later chapters. But that the issues are once again seen as important is abundantly clear.

The argument of this chapter has been to claim that the issues that the Modernists saw as crucial to Christian theology have come back to the centre of contemporary discussion. This suggests that the Modernist approach might have a significant contribution to make once more. That this is so will form the argument of succeeding chapters. But it is important to notice that I talk of the contribution of the Modernist *approach*, rather than of the direct contribution of Modernist writers of the past. This is because the strength of the Modernist writers of the 1920s and 1930s was precisely that they grappled with the best of the modern thought of their own day and sought to relate their Christian beliefs to it. A Modernist theology which seeks to speak to the world at the end of the twentieth century must grapple with the 'modern thought' of its own age. Consequently, I am not going to plead in this book that what we need to do now is to re-read the books written by the Modernists in the 1920s and 1930s. I have encouraged and shall encourage research students to do this, and I have greatly benefited from doing so myself. But in general books with the term 'modern' or 'modernist' in their title succeed best in the age for which they are written.

I hope in the next chapter to show how much contemporary Christianity owes to the Broad Church and Modernist movements of the past century and a half. In doing this I shall indicate that a knowledge of the past history of Christian doctrine such as is disclosed in Hastings Rashdall's work on the Atonement is of great importance in showing why the modernization of belief is necessary.[34] In the chapter on Christology, I shall argue that there are lessons from the debates of the 1920s that we need to relearn in the present. Throughout the book I shall allude to where the 1938 report on doctrine in the Church of England approved or recognized the validity of a Modernist position, and I shall refer to Modernist thinkers wherever their work has continuing relevance. But in general the goal of this book is not to sing the praises of the Modernists of the past, but instead to seek to imitate them in the present. Since 'imitation is the sincerest form of flattery', I hope that I shall in this way disclose my debt to them.

2

Why Modernism was, and is, necessary

The essential claim of Modernist theology is that traditional Christianity needs to be brought up to date and into line with the rest of modern knowledge. For many traditional Christians such a claim is both impertinent and impossible. For they perceive Christianity to be an essentially unchanging revelation given to us by God, and hence by its very nature a faith which we are simply not empowered to change or modify. In recent years those who oppose the ordination of women have largely based their case on such a view of Christianity. For such Christians several biblical texts immediately spring to mind. For example, the Letter of Jude urges its readers to 'join in the struggle for that faith which God entrusted to his people once for all'.[1] Likewise, Hebrews urges its readers to remain loyal to 'God's message' and to remember that 'Jesus Christ is the same yesterday, today and for ever. So do not be swept off your course by all sorts of outlandish teachings'.[2] Other traditionally minded Christians appeal to an unchanging ecclesiastical tradition, remembering that one traditional definition of authentic Christianity, known as the 'Vincentian Canon', says that true faith consists in accepting 'what has been believed everywhere, always, and by all'.[3] Such texts imply an essentially unchanging character to Christian doctrine, and this view is strengthened by the use in public worship of the Apostles' and Nicene Creeds, and by prayers, collects and hymns which often originated many centuries ago. This attitude is not significantly affected by the commissioning of new alternative services, since one criterion in the construction of such services tends to be their conformity with the earliest known forms of Christian worship. The facts that the Church is one of the oldest continuing institutions, that its buildings are frequently the most historic at the centre of town or village, and that bishops and vicars can often trace their predecessors across many centuries, all work together to create a feeling that the Church is or ought to be an unchanging institution guarding a divinely given revelation which also stays the same from age to age.

For those who hold such beliefs any call to 'modernize' their belief-system will be experienced as a threat to it. But others, who are equally committed to the ongoing life of the Church, have come to believe that precisely in order for the continuity of the Church's life to be preserved it must change the expression of its beliefs.This was explicitly the view of the MCU. For many years the *Modern Churchman* quoted the saying of Edmund Burke: 'a State without the means of some change is without the means of its conservation.'[4] It also cited a remark which it attributed to Erasmus: 'By identifying the new learning with heresy you make orthodoxy synonymous with ignorance.'[5] The Modernists took this view partly because they recognized that such developments as biblical criticism and the theory of evolution had to be accepted if Christianity was to remain a credible faith for an informed person, and partly because, as Church historians or experts in the history of Christian doctrine, they were deeply conscious that behind an outward façade of continuity, the way Christianity has been understood has undergone many radical changes throughout its history. An early example of this can be found in Rowland Williams's claim that Christianity should be thought of not as a static religion but as a living faith which has grown and developed as human knowledge advances. Consequently in a succession of generations, 'very great changes may be expected to prevail in the way of expressing Christian truth'.[6]

The most dramatic recent evidence for the very great changes which have taken place in Christianity can be seen in Dennis Nineham's classic work *Christianity, Medieval and Modern,* in which he explores the belief-system of Christians in northern France around the end of the first millennium. Nineham shows conclusively that, despite some familiar features, it would be a 'mistake' to treat this system as if it were 'fundamentally the same religion as ours', for the differences in living religion far outweigh the similarities.[7] For example, tenth-century Frankish Christians perceived everyday life as a battlefield between evil demonic powers, who sought to harm them, and the saints, who were believed to provide defence against such powers as well as against illness and famine. Their whole understanding of the relationship between God and the world was utterly different from that of a modern person.

We do not need to go back to medieval France to see a radically different understanding of Christianity. We merely need to explore the world of our Victorian forebears to realize how differently they understood the Christian message from the way even the most conservative Christian understands it today. To demonstrate this, let us take a thought experiment and travel back in time to the thought-world of the first half of the nineteenth century. The first point we would notice is that almost all Christians assumed that a literal understanding of the Bible was required as an essential basis of faith. As late as 1861, Dean Burgon said of the Bible: 'Every book of it, every chapter of it, every verse of it, every syllable of it, every letter of it, is the direct utterance of the Most High ... faultless, unerring, supreme.'[8] And faultless not merely on matters of religion but also on matters of science, history and morality. Burgon once visited Petra on the Gulf of Aqaba and famously celebrated it as 'A rose-red city – "half as old as time!"'[9] For Burgon that was no poetic fancy but literal truth. Like many Victorians, Burgon owned a Bible which contained in the margin Archbishop Ussher's dating of creation to 4004 BC, and these dates, based on careful working-out of biblical chronology, were taken to be part of the text itself. Consequently, if a city was three thousand years old, it was literally 'half as old as time!' It is hard for us today to imagine what a shortened perspective on antiquity this implied, but for Burgon, and for that half of the clergy who signed their support for his view of the infallibility of the scriptures as late as the 1860s, it was all the history there was or could be.

As well as assuming an infallible Bible, most early Victorians accepted as true a framework of doctrine supposedly taught in it and imbued with an equal infallibility. This doctrinal framework spoke of a literal six-day creation of the world and of Adam and Eve within it. It spoke of their 'original sin' leading to 'the fault and corruption' of human nature, so that every 'person born into this world deserveth God's wrath and damnation' through all eternity.[10] But, according to the 'drama of Salvation', God wanted to save at least some out of this 'mass of perdition' and accordingly sent his Son, Jesus Christ, to die on the cross as 'a sacrifice to atone for and take away the guilt of Adam's original sin, which had so tainted his descendants. Because Jesus was perfect in both divinity and humanity, God accepted the sacrifice of his life as paying the price for human sin. God's anger was averted from those who trusted in Christ alone for their salvation. According to this system of thought, God wanted men and women to know how to identify Christ and so sent prophets to foretell how and where he would be born and the atoning death that he would die. When Jesus came, he perfomed miracles to prove his identity. He was then crucified in accordance with the divine plan, rose from the dead and sent his Spirit on his Church. At the end of time Christ would physically return to earth. The corpses would be reassembled from their graves and raised from the dead. The 'elect' would be carried by the angels to Heaven, while the rest (the vast majority) would be thrown into hell and tortured day and night for ever.[11] This tremendous climax would finally vindicate God's justice and mercy and greatly enhance the bliss of the saved.

Such an outline of Christian belief is so far removed from what even conservative Christians would wish to affirm today that many readers may feel that I have painted a caricature of traditional Christian doctrine. But this is not the case. Detailed exploration shows that it was against precisely such beliefs that Victorian liberals launched their critique. Likewise, studying accounts of Christian doctrine from earlier centuries or exploring traditional liturgy and hymnody will show how deeply rooted such beliefs have been in the Christian tradition. As a former president of the Origen Society, I am of course aware that isolated individual thinkers such as Origen or Peter Abelard or Lady Julian of Norwich can be found throughout the Christian centuries bearing witness to alternative visions. Further, I recognize that the Victorian critique did not emerge out of the blue but was in some ways prefigured by the ideas of the Cambridge Platonists of the seventeenth century and by the Latitudinarian mentality of many Anglican theologians and philosophers of the eighteenth-century 'Age of Reason'.

Yet, despite such qualifications, the fact remains that the systematic doctrine of the fall and redemption of man was what most Victorian Christians understood Christianity to be, and that for most of the Christian centuries the 'drama of salvation' has been at the heart of Christian preaching. Belief in the infallibility of scripture and the literal truth of a six-day creation was a largely unquestioned assumption from the earliest days of the faith. Belief in the 'fall' of Adam and Eve was axiomatic to Pauline theology, and a developed understanding of 'original sin' goes back at least to St Augustine. Similarly, the idea that the Old Testament prophets had foretold the coming of Christ is found explicitly both in St Matthew's Gospel and in the Acts of the Apostles, while the seeing of miracles as 'signs' of Christ's true nature and mission is a theme of St John's Gospel. A developed understanding of substitition atonement goes back at least to St Anselm, replacing an understanding of Christ's death as a ransom paid to the Devil which had been widely believed earlier. A full-blooded doctrine of hell-fire is taken for granted in the book of Revelation and dominated the Christian imagination until the middle of the nineteenth century. What is even worse is that the 'abominable fancy' that one of the greatest joys of heaven was to watch the damned being tortured is implied in Revelation 14: 10, was explicitly taught by Tertullian around the year 200 CE,[12] and has been endorsed by many leading Christian saints and theologians ever since. According to Peter Lombard's influential textbook, 'the elect shall go forth ... to see the torments of the impious, and seeing this they will not be affected by grief, but will be satiated with joy at the sight of their unutterable calamity'.[13] St Thomas Aquinas wrote that 'in order that the happiness of the saints may be more delightful to them and that they may render more copious thanks to God, a perfect view of the sufferings of the damned is granted to them'.[14]

Almost all contemporary Christians accept that, taken as a totality, this belief-system, though assumed by the vast majority of Christians right up to the Victorian era, is no longer credible. As one leading Modernist scholar, Canon J. S. Bezzant, put it: 'known facts of astronomy, geology, biological evolution, anthropology, the comparative study of religions, race and genetical and analytic psychology, the literary and historical criticism of the Bible, with the teaching of Jesus and the moral conscience of mankind, have banished this scheme beyond the range of credibility'.[15] The reason that the traditional 'drama of salvation' became untenable was simply that astronomy and geology shattered the Genesis timescale,[16] while biological evolution and anthropology showed that the human race was not created perfect, but gradually developed from a sub-human past. Hence the concept of an original sin damaging pristine virtue became untenable.[17] The rise of historical and literary criticism in classical studies, and the subsequent application of this methodology to biblical studies, revealed that the prophets of Israel should be understood as men who proclaimed the will of God to their own day, rather than as soothsayers of a far-distant Messianic future.[18] Likewise, the new study of comparative religion showed that the attribution of miraculous powers to charismatic religious leaders was a common feature of human religious experience, and hence the telling of such stories about Jesus could in no way be considered as evidence of any divine status for him.[19]

Finally, the emergence of autonomous ethical judgement in Kant's description of the categorical imperative, or in the rise of Utilitarian principles propounded by James Mill and Jeremy Bentham, provided standpoints from which it was possible to call into question the morality of parts of the Old Testament, and of elements within the Christian drama of salvation.[20] Modern research has shown that the rise of an autonomous ethic was the major factor in the Victorian crisis of faith, as the morality of original sin, of vicarious atonement and, above all, of endless torment in hell was challenged by people who felt that they had a higher ethic than that displayed in the version of Christianity being proclaimed to them.[21]

One consequence of this was that the Victorian crisis of faith was one of the most traumatic periods of human religious history. As Alec Vidler puts it:

> nearly all the representatives of Victorian religious thought, nearly all the intellectuals had to struggle with religious belief ... Never has any age in history produced such a detailed literature of lost faith or of so many great men and women of religious temperament standing outside organised religion.[22]

As Vidler indicates, the complete abandonment of Christianity was one way of responding to the discrediting of the old schema. But the pioneers of Modernist theology showed that there was an alternative. The trail was blazed by Friedrich Schleiermacher, who realized that his own personal consciousness of God had not

been affected by his abandonment of belief in the system of theology in which he had grown up. What mattered for religious
feeling was personal religious experience. His own experience had
been initially nourished by his reading of the Bible and by the
fellowship he had experienced within the Moravian Church, but
it did not depend on continued acceptance of their doctrinal
system or of an unjustified belief in biblical infallibility. As the
beliefs of his childhood vanished before his doubting eyes, the
religious sense remained.[23] From this experience, Schleiermacher
went on to reinterpret the Christian message on the basis that its
truest foundation was the living Christian experiencing of his
own generation.[24] S. T. Coleridge visited Germany just after
Schleiermacher's speeches *On Religion* had been published, and
brought back to Britain this new approach to Christian theology.
Almost all the Modernists refer to Coleridge as one of the major
influences on the origin of their movement. Coleridge stressed the
experiential foundation for living faith. He showed that a deep
commitment to the inspiration of the Bible was fully compatible
with recognition of errors within it, and that faith in Christ was
in no way dependent on belief in such things as original sin,
substitution atonement, or hell.[25]

F. D. Maurice took this approach much further. He claimed
that such beliefs were not merely inessential to Christianity, they
were incompatible with it. Maurice believed that the erosion of
faith among his contemporaries was a direct result of a 'mon-
strous perversion' of Christianity being proclaimed in place of the
original Gospel.[26] For the doctrines of original sin, substitution
atonement, and hell are in direct contradiction to the primal and
quite decisive Christian doctrine of the love of God. If we start
from belief that 'God is actually love', we shall 'dread any representation of Him which is at variance with this [and] will shrink
from attributing to Him acts which would be unlovely in man'.[27]

From this premiss Maurice argued that the idea that a historical
fall had led to the total depravity of human nature was 'a horrible
notion which has haunted moralists, divines and practical men',
and runs directly contrary to the New Testament's teaching that sin
is *not* part of our nature but something that we are all called to fight
against.[28] Moreover, if anyone believes that Christ is 'the light
which enlightens every man who comes into the world',[29] he
cannot also believe that humankind is of necessity depraved.

Consequently, to believe in a historical fall is a 'most flagrant denial of God'.[30]

Maurice claimed likewise that any doctrine of the atonement which presumes that sins cannot be forgiven unless satisfaction is first paid also contradicts the teaching of Jesus; as Maurice puts it, 'We can forgive a fellow-creature a wrong done to us, without exacting an equivalent for it. We think we are offending against Christ's command who said, "Be ye merciful as your Father in heaven is merciful" if we do not.'[31] Maurice believed that the whole notion of Christ having to die in order to appease God's anger was completely contrary to the doctrine of Christ's incarnation, that 'God was in Christ reconciling the world to himself'.[32] Consequently, according to Maurice, 'Orthodox faith as it is expressed in the Bible and the Creeds absolutely prevents us from acquiescing in some of those explanations of the Atonement which both in popular and scholastic teachings have been identified with it.'[33] 'If we would adhere to the faith once for all delivered to the saints we must not dare to speak of Christ as changing that Will which he took flesh and died to fulfil.'[34]

Finally, Maurice taught that the doctrine of hell made a mockery of Jesus' picture of the loving fatherhood of God. For if it were indeed the case that all humanity is damned except those who accept Christ as their personal saviour, it would condemn 'most of the American slaves, and the whole body of Turks, Hindus, Hottentots and Jews ... to hopeless destruction from which a few persons, some of whom are living comfortably without any vexation of heart, may by special mercy be delivered'.[35] Such a conclusion would negate belief in the infinite love of our heavenly Father and utterly destroy the credibility of the Christian Gospel.

I have focused on F. D. Maurice partly because he demonstrated most fully the incompatibility of key features of the traditional framework of salvation with the central themes of Jesus' teaching concerning the love of God, and partly because he is the nineteenth-century figure most often appealed to by the twentieth century. But many other writers made important additional contributions. Benjamin Jowett wrote a detailed commentary on St Paul's Epistles in which he showed that the doctrine of substitution atonement was read into rather than out of the Pauline text and that the doctrine was scarcely known in the first thousand years of the Christian era.[36] Rowland Williams showed that to think of the Old Testament prophets simply as visionaries of a long-distant future was wholly to misunderstand their works and to veil the profound moral and religious value of their actual teaching.[37] And S. R. Driver claimed that to see Genesis as a putative scientific textbook was to fail to appreciate the kind of literature it actually was.

In similar vein, Aubrey Moore argued that there were positive religious gains in accepting the theory of evolution. Writing in 1889, he claimed that prior to the rise of evolutionary theory the Christian understanding of divine creation had gradually been reduced to little more than belief in a deistic absentee God who, having initally created the world, thereafter took little interest in it. This notion Moore believed had been undermined by the theory of evolution:

> Darwinism appeared and under the guise of a foe did the work of a friend . . . by showing us that . . . God is everywhere present in nature or He is nowhere. It seems as if, in the providence of God, the mission of modern science was to bring home to us . . . the great truth of the Divine immanence in creation which is essential to a Christian view.[38]

What all this adds up to is that the belief-system taken for granted by almost all Christians throughout the ages of faith had become impossible for educated Christians to accept by the end of the nineteenth century. But this was not then widely recognized within the Church as a whole. Hence, liberal Christians felt themselves at risk in challenging the traditional viewpoint. Because of this the Modern Churchmen's Union was founded in 1898 under the initial title of The Churchmen's Union for the Advancement of Liberal Religious Thought. The first objective of the Union was 'to unite Churchmen who consider that dogma is capable of re-interpretation and restatement in accordance with the clearer perception of truth attained by discovery and research'. In 1902 this was changed to 'to maintain the right and duty of the Church to restate her belief from time to time as required by the progressive revelation of the Holy Spirit'. In 1910 the journal *The Modern Churchman* was founded, and in 1932 the Churchmen's Union incorporated the word 'Modern' into its formal title. It also expanded the original first objective into five clauses:

1. To affirm the progressive character of God's self-revelation, and the certainty that no truth can lead away from Him.
2. To proclaim Christ and his Gospel in the light of modern knowledge, endeavouring to give a clear meaning to all phrases which are open to ambiguous treatment.
3. To maintain the right and duty of the Church of England to reject what is false and restate what is true in her traditional dogmas.
4. To defend the freedom of responsible students, clerical as well as lay, in their work of criticism and research.
5. To promote the study of the Bible according to modern critical methods and to interpret its message in the light of such study.[39]

From the perspective of today, such objectives could be endorsed by almost any contemporary Christian. The principle of the historico-critical study of the Bible is axiomatic in all university departments of theology, colleges of higher education, and school syllabuses. Evangelical and Catholic scholars alike see the need to use such methodology to defend their positions. Likewise, the progressive character of revelation is almost universally accepted, in that not even the most conservative Christian would feel totally bound by Old Testament law. For example, though some Evangelicals feel bound to accept the Old Testament condemnation of homosexuality, none accept the further requirement of the Old Testament law that it must be punished by death. Similarly, all accept that the Church has a right and duty to reject what is false and restate what is true in traditional doctrine. The clearest example of this is the formal repudiation of everlasting torment in hell by the Doctrine Commission of the Church of England.[40]

With hindsight we can see that what the Broad Church thinkers of the nineteenth century and their Modernist successors in the twentieth did was to make it intellectually possible to be a Christian today. Writing in 1964, Alec Vidler acknowledged that he had had a negative attitude towards Modernism for as long as he could remember but had more recently changed his attitude towards it because 'I have come to suspect that throughout my lifetime it has done much more than any other version of Christian faith to enable ordinary people – as distinct from sophisticated theologians – to continue to be professing Christians'.[41] They did this by showing that belief in God, in Christ, in spirituality and in the life of the world to come could be divorced from belief in the traditional framework of salvation. This achievement has become permanent because, although phrases from the old schema still occur in liturgy, hymns and sermons, such phrases are now separated from the system of thought to which they once belonged.

For example, although festivals of lessons and carols continue to use the traditional 'messianic' passages from the Old Testament as foretelling the coming of Christ, no scholar imagines that this was the original meaning of such passages. Likewise, although the 'fall' continues to be referred to, few if any scholars believe that it relates to some actual aboriginal historical event. And, although preachers may still talk of our 'being saved', they do not specify that it is from 'God's wrath and everlasting damnation' that we are to be saved! Instead the phraseology has floated free from the structured belief-system of which it was once part and now seems to refer to a 'feel-good' factor associated with a decision to commit oneself to Christ. For it is apparent that, with the rejection of hell, there is no damnation to be saved from, and there is a widespread acceptance even in evangelical circles that eternal salvation is fully open to those who have rejected Christ. This can be illustrated by the decision of the Archbishop of Canterbury to pray for Princess Diana's Islamic lover Dodi al Fayed, 'in certain hope of resurrection to eternal life',[42] and that this prayer attracted no comment even though the funeral service was heard by more people across the world than any other broadcast in history.

The case for Modernist theology can be summed up by observing that the traditional framework of Christian belief is almost universally accepted as being no longer factually true. This means that if Christianity is to continue to exist as a credible belief-system, a new way must be found to articulate its central message in ways which cohere with the rest of our knowledge and well-founded beliefs about reality. This is what Modernist theologians have sought to do for the past hundred years, and I shall seek to give a brief sketch of what such a picture might be like in the second half of this book. But before turning to this, I must first explore the alternative responses to the crisis of modernity that have replaced the Modernist agenda in contemporary theology.

3

Modernism in relation to Neo-orthodoxy

The essential claim of Modernist theology is that if Christianity is to be a serious intellectual option for an educated contemporary person, it is vital that its belief-system should be compatible with what the sciences tell us about the nature of reality, with what we experience as important in our lives, with what historical research tells us about the nature of the biblical record, and with what our moral judgement tells us is acceptable for us to believe and practise today. This does not mean that Christians are bound to accept whatever happens to be the current consensus among contemporary scientists, psychologists, historians or moralists. Much of modern intellectual life is very secularized and does not always take into account considerations which are crucial to the religious believer. But a Modernist would argue that a Christian scholar ought to be able to show that her or his religious beliefs are at least compatible with their other beliefs. The philosophical premiss of Modernism is belief in the unity of knowledge. It presupposes that any propositional statement whatever can only be true if it is compatible with other knowledge or well-founded beliefs that we have about the nature of reality, and that this presupposition applies just as much to the claims of religion as to any other claims.

Modernism is therefore very distinct from other theological positions in existence today. In particular, it differs from contemporary Neo-orthodoxy in insisting that religious beliefs which claim to be derived from revelation cannot be isolated from the rest of our knowledge or be given immunity from the demands of the correspondence theory of truth. Modernism also differs from existentialist, post-Modern or non-realist versions of Christianity in making claims about God, Christ, spirituality and life after death which challenge the basic pre-understandings of secular thought. It is therefore open to attack from both radical and conservative perspectives, and as a theological system it has long been regarded as outmoded by both of them. To suggest that it offers a 'contemporary challenge' is thus to throw down a gauntlet to dominant movements in much twentieth-century Christian thought.

The most basic reason for the eclipse of Modernism in the last fifty years is that for most of this period the intellectual presuppositions which undergirded it have been generally discounted. To suppose that scientific and philosophical considerations are relevant to belief is to make a claim about Natural Theology, and for much of the past fifty years Natural Theology has been regarded with the gravest suspicion. The fullest and best defence of Natural Theology by a Modernist scholar is F. R. Tennant's work *Philosophical Theology*, published in two volumes in 1927 and 1928.[1] It was an immediate success and was reprinted in 1935. But, despite containing a penetrating understanding of the role of religious experience in shaping the human psyche, as well as a defence of the argument from design which can still contribute to the contemporary debate, Tennant's work became increasingly ignored because the current of intellectual thought ceased to flow in that direction. The publication of Sigmund Freud's work *The Future of an Illusion* in 1928[2] persuaded many that alternative pathological explanations could be given for religious experience from the perspective of analytical psychology. The year 1936 saw the publication of A. J. Ayer's youthful firework *Language, Truth and Logic*,[3] which heralded the birth of logical positivism in philosophy, in which religious affirmations were seen as literally 'non-sense'. And 1938 saw the publication of Karl Barth's Gifford Lectures; in these he argued against the theological legitimacy of any appeal to Natural Theology[4] and made the British public conscious of the new movement in theology which Barth epitomized and which increasingly came to dominate theological discussion.

A similar development took place in biblical studies, where the growth of form-criticism persuaded at least two generations of New Testament scholars that we can say very little with confidence about the historical Jesus. This conviction undermined the Modernist premiss that the core of authentic Christianity could be identified with what historical research about 'Jesus and his Gospel'. Hence to try and bring Christianity back to the 'original' message of its founder (as the Modernists of the Girton Conference of 1921 had sought to do) was an impossibility. This undermined another of the basic premises of classic Modernism.

The credibility of Modernism today must depend to a great extent on whether or not the premises on which the Modernists originally built can be restored. Hence, the discussion in subsequent chapters of the impact of the 'new physics' on belief in God, and of recent historical research on what we can justifiably say about the Jesus of History, is crucial to the argument of this book. The most basic reason for Modernism's eclipse was that in general Christian theologians ceased to start from the same premises as the Modernists, and hence inevitably reached different conclusions. The conclusion one comes to on any issue will largely depend on the pre-understanding from which one starts. A theologian who believes that Natural Theology is either impossible or illegitimate will naturally end up with a very different understanding of the rationale for Christian belief from one who assumes the validity of Natural Theology. Likewise, a theologian who thinks that the historical Jesus is opaque to us will inevitably emphasize instead the role of Christ as proclaimed in the life of the Church. Hence, although in this chapter and the next I shall criticize what I see as weaknesses in some other theological movements, whether or not they really are weaknesses will largely depend on the validity of the arguments to be presented later relating to Natural Theology and what we can legitimately claim to know about Jesus.

In the history of thought Modernism was eclipsed by the towering influence of Karl Barth, and to this day the Barthian rejection of liberal theology remains so powerful a force that, unless Barth can be shown to be wrong, it cannot be re-established. I believe it is therefore necessary for me to give extensive coverage to Barth's views and to the difficulties that I see as inherent in them.

Barth was thoroughly acquainted with liberal theological thought, at least in its German form. He wrote *Protestant Theology in the Nineteenth Century* (1946),[5] which has become a standard history. He was perennially fascinated with the thought of Friedrich Schleiermacher, 'the father of modern theology', and among his own theological tutors was Adolf von Harnack, the very epitome of the Liberal Protestant tradition, and one of the greatest influences on English Modernism. Barth's rejection of liberal theology was based not on any misunderstanding of what it taught, but on a profound conviction that it was wrong.

Barth's rejection of Natural Theology was absolute, not only because, like most German Protestant theologians, he believed that Kant had definitively destroyed all the classic arguments for the existence of God, but, more importantly, because he believed that whenever theologians sought to integrate theology with scientific and philosophical thinking, theology always ended up playing second fiddle. The Word of God was made subordinate to the word of man, and what one was allowed to think theologically was restricted to what the dominant philosophy of the day regarded as 'possible'. Barth believed that the weakness of this approach had been exposed by the early nineteenth-century Danish thinker Søren Kierkegaard. Kierkegaard had argued that the liberal thinkers of his day had 'watered down' Christianity until it wholly conformed with the requirements of Hegelian philosophy. It left out everything distinctive about the message of salvation and the experience of redemption through the cross of Christ. It ignored the fundamental difference between God and man and gave no heed to the utter transcendence and total 'otherness' of God.

Barth believed that a similar weakness existed in all attempts to base Christianity on religious experience. Schleiermacher and his successors had sought to find a foundation for religious belief in human 'feeling' or the intuitions of the human heart. Schleiermacher believed that religious consciousness was the one foundation on which first-hand faith could be based, and in his greatest work, *The Christian Faith*, he tried to show that the whole of Christian doctrine was derivable from the religious consciousness of the contemporary Christian community. Barth believed that the danger of such a view was that one ended up identifying Christianity with the culture of one's own day. Barth saw this exemplified in the decision of a well-known German liberal theologian, Ernst

Troeltsch, to move in 1914 from the chair of Systematic Theology at Heidelberg to a chair in the History and Philosophy of Civilization at Berlin. Much more significantly, however, Barth believed that the weakness of 'Culture Protestantism' was further exposed in August 1914, when Adolf von Harnack and other German intellectuals issued a statement in support of the Kaiser's war policy. To his horror, Barth saw the names of almost all his theological teachers whom he had greatly revered. Fearful of what this meant, he felt he could follow neither their theology nor their ethics. For Barth, liberal theology no longer had a future. If the theologians of his day could not see that the war was an act of madness and folly, they clearly were blind guides, and a wholly new approach to theology was needed. This moral conviction of the inadequacy of a 'culture Protestantism' which swims with the tide of the rest of human thought was further exemplified for Barth later in his career, when he realized that the 'Faith Movement of German Christians' was ready to assimilate Christianity into the ideology of Nazism. The official Church leadership could make no adequate response to it, and went along with the resurgence of German nationalism. Barth saw this as the logical consequence of a century and a half of assimilating Christianity to whatever happened to be the dominant thought of the day. This culture Protestantism might seem harmless when it was simply a question of assimilating Christianity to philosophical idealism, but when it came to assimilating Christianity to Nazism the disaster of such a policy was fully exposed.

Barth believed that the only secure foundation for Christian doctrine was a theology of revelation breaking in perpendicularly from above. He believed that from the human side there was no point of contact between man and God. 'Natural Theology', so far from giving any authentic knowledge, is described by Barth as 'the great temptation and source of all error in theology. It comes from anti-Christ and is to be turned away at the threshold.'[6] Likewise, Barth believed that faith is not to be derived from human religious experiencing, which he thought of as a 'a mode of unbelief' which 'bolts and bars' the way to an acceptance of revelation.[7] Everything that is called religion 'from the grossest superstition to the most delicate spirituality, from naked rationalism to the most subtle mysticism – remains on this side of the abyss'.[8] Only the miracle of revelation can give any knowledge of God. This revelation comes to us through the Church's proclamation of Jesus Christ.

Barth believed that revelation was embodied in the *Credo* of the Church, which has to be accepted as an objective given: 'A science of faith which denied or even questioned the faith of the Church would cease to be either "faithful" or "scientific".'[9] Barth believed that theology is simply 'Faith seeking Understanding'. it comes from acceptance of what is preached as true, for 'the Word of Christ is identical with the "Word of those who preach Christ"'.[10] According to Barth any authentic representation of the Word would 'include the Bible in a very special way', but he thought that the Bible can never be properly understood except in relation to the *Credo* of the Church. The Bible itself is simply a 'literary monument of an ancient racial religion and of a Hellenistic cultus religion of the Near East. A human document like any other.'[11] In many ways the Bible is a very strange and alien book. Nevertheless, through 'the miracle of faith' we can hear God speaking to us in the Bible in his self-disclosure in Christ. What matters in this self-disclosure, however, is not Jesus 'according to the flesh', for the earthly Jesus was 'either an apocalyptic fanatic or the divine incognito'.[12] The revelation consists in the credal affirmations concerning the incarnation, crucifixion and resurrection of the Son of God, through which was 'legally re-established the covenant between God and man', and through which came 'the promise of our eternal life'.[13]

Barth compared himself to a man stumbling in a bell-tower who, reaching out for a banister, seized a rope and discovered that he had rung a bell to which many responded. His thought was immediately perceived as having an important message and as a turning-point in the history of twentieth-century theology. As the disaster of the First World War was followed by the economic collapse of Germany and then by the rise of Nazism, the old Calvinistic doctrine of the total depravity of humanity without Christ seemed common sense. Within Germany it became extremely important that Barth drafted the Barmen declaration of 1934, which formed the title deeds of the 'Confessing Church', the one organization that provided at least some kind of opposition during the years of Nazi tyranny. It came to be widely believed that Barthian theology was the only version of Christianity which could take an independent stand, and as the theology of the Confessing Church it possessed great moral authority in the post-war years. Barth came to be seen not only as a great theologian, but also as a twentieth-century prophet proclaiming the righteousness of God. For Christians in Germany, reverence for Barth was associated with a belief that his theology had given Germany back its soul after the betrayals of the Nazi era, and John Bowden vividly documents with what great expectations each new volume of his *Church Dogmatics* was awaited there.[14]

However, there are very serious problems in seeing a doctrine of revelation as providing the solution to the challenge of modernity. The most obvious is the problem of how to identify what the revelation is. As we have seen, Barth is not a Biblical fundamentalist, and nor does he embrace the whole of the Christian tradition. He makes a personal selection from the corpus of beliefs which Christians have held and identifies his selection as being what the revelation teaches. As a Modernist, I have every sympathy with such a procedure, which seems to me unavoidable if one is to present Christianity in a way which makes sense in the modern world. But what I do not understand is how such selectivity can be justified within a tradition that claims to be bound by a God-given revelation which must eschew the temptation to relate itself to other learning. One cannot legitimately claim the authority of a divine revelation breaking in perpendicularly from above if ones makes a highly personal choice out of what the Bible and the Church have taught, and if one then goes on to give an extremely creative and original interpretation to some of these beliefs. Yet this in fact is what Barth does.

A related issue is whether or not a culture-free understanding of revelation is actually possible. How would such a revelation be understood or accepted if there were not already a pre-existing language and world-view which would enable the revelation to be received and accepted? Even the claim that God revealed himself in Christ is only intelligible if the person who hears the claim has a pre-existing understanding of what the words 'God', 'Christ' and 'revelation' mean. As we shall see later, such considerations raise very serious difficulties for the whole of Barth's system. For the present, however, let us observe that it is by no means clear that Barth's political views necessarily stemmed from his theological convictions. In his writings he makes much of the fact that some leading theological liberals were so bound up with the cultural assumptions of the German ruling class that they supported the war-aims of the Kaiser, and that later the association of the Lutheran Church with German nationhood made it blind to the horrors of Nazi racism. But did Barth's opposition to such views really stem from his theology, or from the fact that his own cultural formation was the product of his Swiss nationality? Barth was a Swiss pastor living and working in a country where ethnic Germans, Italians and French had for centuries shared a sense of Swiss nationhood and culture and had lived together in peace and harmony. For any citizen of Switzerland it must indeed have seemed extraordinary that war should break out between France, Germany and Italy. Likewise, it is not surprising that a person whose historical understanding was shaped by the ideals of Swiss democracy should feel appalled by the *Führer* principle, and should argue strongly that a Christian should only give the title 'leader' to Christ.

Looking back from the eve of a third millennium it becomes apparent that Barth's theology was as culturally conditioned as any other human theology. It grew out of an anti-Semitic, monocultural and patriarchal environment and is only intelligible in that context. The anti-Semitic element in Barth tends to be ignored because of his role in the foundation of the Confessing Church, because of his condemnation of Nazi persecution, and because of his efforts to aid Jewish immigration from the Nazi-occupied territories. He preached a famous sermon in which he reminded his hearers that 'Jesus Christ was a Jew', and in a private letter afterwards said that no Christian should be involved in the 'ill-treatment of the Jews which is now the order of the day'.[15] Yet despite all this, what strikes the reader fifty years on is how much Barth had in common with his opponents. It is extraordinary that though the Barmen declaration of 1934 was triggered by a Nazi rule forbidding the ordination of baptized Jews to the Christian ministry, the Barmen declaration itself makes no explicit reference to the plight of the Jews, but is solely concerned with confessional purity and the freedom of the Church from State interference. In 1967 Barth admitted that he had 'long felt guilty' about not making 'the Jewish problem' central or at least public' in the Barmen documents.[16]

But the problem for Barth is that one of the premisses on which his whole theological system is built is that Jesus Christ is the only way to knowledge of God. Hence, he could not accept that Jews, who had explicitly rejected Christ, could have any authentic knowledge of God. Yet wholly to dismiss the reality of the Jewish knowledge of God is the most profoundly anti-Semitic accusation one can make against a religious Jew. Barth always believed that Israel had been displaced by Christianity: 'the people of God were first Israel and later the Church'.[17] Barth speaks of the 'evil history of these disobedient people' and of 'the guilt of Jewry, manifest in the Synagogue combating the Church'.[18] He even suggested that the Holocaust was a judgement of God on them, 'a result of their unfaithfulness'.[19]

In fairness to Barth, a key element in his commentary on the Epistle to the Romans is that even these sinful, lost and disobedient people will ultimately share in the redemption wrought by Christ.[20] But this does not take away the fact that his theology presupposes the displacement of Judaism by Christianity, and the total inauthenticity of contemporary Jewish religious life. What this means is that, although Barth opposed the policies the Nazis adopted towards the Jews, he breathed new life into the kind of theology that paved the way for its emergence. Any theology of revelation which says that there can be no knowledge of God at all apart from Jesus Christ will inevitably be hostile to the religion out of which Christianity came but of whose members a majority did not accept Christ.

Barth's rejection of Judaism highlights the wider problem that Barth lived in an overwhelmingly Christian or post-Christian culture and knew little if anything of people of other religions. This cultural situation decisively influenced his theological thinking. He was able to believe that non-Christians have no knowledge of God at all because he had never met a person of another faith to whom God was profoundly real. This became clear from a meeting Barth had with an Indian Christian, D. T.

Niles, in 1935. According to Dr Gavin D' Costa:

> Barth asserted that 'other religions are just unbelief'. Niles
> replied, asking, 'How many Hindus, Dr Barth, have you met?'
> Barth's unhesitating reply was 'Not one'. To this Niles pressed
> the issue a little further: 'How then do you know that Hinduism
> is unbelief?' Barth's answer, which took Niles by surprise, was
> quite simply 'A priori!'[21]

The problem with such a perspective is precisely its *a priori* character. Once one has come to know a single devout person of another
theistic faith, such an attitude becomes impossible. Barth's premiss
that 'God can only be known in Christ' is dependent on a fundamental ignorance of the extra-Christian religious experience of the
human race. In a pluralist society like modern Britain it is the most
obvious weakness with a theology of revelation. As one who
teaches in a multi-religious department of Theology and Religious
Studies, it has become embarrassing to lecture on Barth, because
present in the lecture room will be at least some non-Christian
students whose total dedication to God is a standing denial of
Barth's ignorant assertion.

An equivalent problem arises from Barth's attitude to women
and to homosexuality, where it is clear that the perspective
expressed in his *Church Dogmatics* simply reflects the cultural
assumptions of the 1930s couched in theological language. Thus
Barth affirms that 'God's command uncompromisingly requires
of [man and woman] the observance of divine order in their relationship'. In this divine ordering the man should always 'take
precedence ... as the one who leads and inspires', while the
woman will accept 'her subordinate role' and 'be obedient' to
him, 'realising that her own independence honour and dignity ...
are best secured ... within the precedence she sees man assume'.[22]
Concerning what Barth calls 'the malady called homosexuality',
he describes this as 'the physical, psychological, and social sick-
ness, the phenomenon of perversion, decadence and decay, which
can emerge when man refuses to admit the validity of the divine
command'.[23] From the perspective of the new millennium, one
can see that what Barth identified as part of divine revelation
could more aptly be described as the prejudices of an earlier age.
Certainly no feminist could read Barth's discussion of the proper

relationship between men and women without squirming at the way he takes for granted the givenness of male superiority. And, likewise, no homosexual could read Barth's comments without identifying a serious case of homophobia. This highlights the problem of any theology based on divine revelation: that people find it incredibly hard to distinguish what authentically comes from God from what is manifestly derived from human tradition. In a Modernist perspective this problem does not arise, since it is axiomatic to Modernism that all knowledge of God comes through the responses of fallible human beings. But it is fatal to Barthian claims about a revelation breaking in perpendicularly from above and free from all contact with human culture that so much of what Barth claimed as part of that revelation is so manifestly dependent on the cultural traditions of his day.

There is also the problem of the relationship between Barth's ethics and his own personal life. Barth wrote at immense length on the proper relationship between man and woman and of 'the fundamental law of love and marriage', and says that 'if we are to be obedient to the divine command we cannot regard ourselves as dispensed from its observance'.[24] Yet for sixteen years prior to writing this passage, and for at least as many after writing it, Barth seems to have followed a totally different way of life from that which his theological writings prescribed for him. As Eberhard Busch's biography makes clear, Barth's closest companion was not his wife, but another woman whom he introduced into his household and who remained for over thirty years. According to Busch:

many good friends, and not least his mother, took offence at the presence of 'Lollo' in Barth's life and later in his home. There is no question that the intimacy of her relationship with him made particularly heavy demands on the patience of his wife Nelly. Now she had to retreat into the background. Nevertheless she did not forsake her husband ... It was very difficult indeed for the three of them to live together. Barth did not hesitate to take the responsibility and the blame for the situation which had come about. But he thought it could not be changed ... the result was that they bore a burden which caused them unspeakably deep suffering. Tensions arose which shook them to the core ... In addition to the many events of the following decades

Karl Barth, his wife and Charlotte von Kirchbaum also had to keep struggling to sustain and to tolerate their burden and the tensions it produced. Nor should it be forgotten that Barth's children each in their own way also faced the burden of this difficulty at home and suffered under it.[25]

I have no wish to make any comment on the tragedy of another human being's life except to marvel that his own experiencing had so little effect on his writing that he could continue to write about the absolute priority of living in obedience to the divine commands while forcing his wife to live in a hell-on-earth situation.

Barth's political judgement is also thrown into doubt by his attitude towards Communism. It was a constant surprise to his contemporaries that one who was so clear-sighted about the evils of Hitlerism should be blind to the equal or greater evils of Stalinism. But it seems that Barth's own early commitment to Christian Socialism made him view what was happening in Eastern Europe through rose-coloured spectacles. He always insisted that 'anti-Communism was a greater evil than Communism', and his stance did much to influence the way the World Council of Churches did so little to highlight the problems being faced by Christians behind the Iron Curtain.[26] From the perspective of history, Barth's prophetic insight looks much more dubious than it appeared at the time of the Barmen declaration and shows how difficult it is to maintain that a theology of revelation can bring greater political insight than any other system.

The deepest problem with Barthianism has yet to be addressed. This is the problem of what meaning can really be given to theological terminology when it is explicitly divorced from human reason, knowledge and experience. The main reason for the appeal of Barthian theology was that it encouraged generations of clergy to believe that they could ignore the problems raised by the nineteenth century and could once more preach with confidence on the great themes of historical orthodoxy. They could speak confidently of God, of Christ, of creation and the fall, of the work of Christ in our redemption, and the good news of his resurrection. I vividly remember the sense of exhilaration I felt as a young theologian in reading Barth's exuberant confidence in the self-validating power of theology and the truth of the Christian proclamation. But I have come to believe that there are fatal difficulties with his position which simply have to be faced. The challenge of modern knowledge cannot be overcome by a unilateral declaration of independence by theology, because when theological language is wholly removed from ordinary language it ceases to carry its original meaning.

Consider, for example, what happens to belief in God as creator if one takes seriously Barth's position that Natural Theology must be totally eschewed because theology and science operate in 'two fundamentally distinct spheres' so that 'dogmatics has no business to broaden out into cosmology' and is 'fundamentally free in regard to all world-pictures, that is, to all attempts to regard what exists by the measure and with the means of the dominant science of the time'.[27] On this basis Barth felt free to expound the biblical view of creation through an exposition of Genesis 1 and 2, without feeling any sense of obligation to relate this to such things as the theories of evolution and relativity. Against this Modernism claims that there cannot be two realities. We cannot genuinely hold on Sundays a different set of beliefs from those we assume on a day-to-day basis about the nature of reality. If our religious beliefs have no connection with our other beliefs, then it is questionable whether they even exist as authentic beliefs. When Langdon Gilkey claims that religious truth is effectively removed 'from the area of matters of fact',[28] I find myself baffled to know what the words 'religious truth' can then mean. The claim that 'God created the universe' is only meaningful if one is talking about the actual cosmos which scientists investigate, and making a claim that ultimately God is responsible for its existence. On this point the Modernists were completely clear. According to Henry Major, 'The Modernist believes in God working in and through the creative process [and] ... as existing before and independently of the created universe.'[29] We shall see later that this is precisely the line taken by many Christian scholars today in the tremendous revival of Natural Theology in our own day. For the present let us simply note the views of perhaps the most distinguished contemporary German theologian, Wolfhart Pannenberg:

If the God of the Bible is creator of the universe then it is not possible to understand fully or even appropriately the processes of nature without reference to that God. If, on the contrary, nature can be appropriately understood without reference to the God of the Bible, then that God cannot be the creator of the universe, and consequently could not be truly God.[30]

A second problem with Barth's understanding of God and creation is that he constantly insists that we can know nothing of either except through Christ. 'We know God in Jesus Christ alone',[31] so that 'God is unknown to us at our Father or as the Creator to the extent that he is not known through Jesus'.[32] This *apparently* high Christology of Barth has had an enormous influence on Christian thought, but I speak deliberately of an *apparently* high Christology here, because when Christological claims are pushed to such extremes as Barth pushes them they become empty of all meaning. After all, if it were literally true that 'We know God through Jesus Christ alone', then to say 'God was in Christ' would actually not mean anything. If we really had *no* knowledge of God outside our knowledge of Jesus, then to say 'Jesus is God' would become equivalent to uttering the tautology 'Jesus is Jesus'. The sentence 'Jesus is God' only adds anything to our knowledge of Jesus if the word 'God' has meaning apart from him. An even deeper problem with Barth's theology is to know what meaning one is to attach to talk of God if there is nothing in human reasoning or experience for the concept to latch on to. If we suppose it to be really true that 'Without Jesus we can say nothing at all about God and man and their relationship with one another', how does this situation existentially differ from atheism? If both atheist and Barthian agree that there is nothing in human reasoning or in human experiencing which could justify belief in God, does the fact that a Barthian claims to believe that events in Palestine two thousand years ago revealed God then make any significant difference to their different world-views now?

The situation is even more perplexing when we consider that, although Barth talks constantly about 'Jesus Christ', to the extent that his theology is often described as Christomonist, Barth was, on his own admission, 'frightfully indifferent'[33] to what we can actually know about the historical Jesus 'according to the flesh', for the earthly Jesus was 'either an apocalyptic fanatic or the divine incognito'.[34] Barth thinks that we can know very little about the life of Jesus and that the little we do know does not really commend him to us. Barth is quite scathing about the 'uncritical equanimity' with which Jesus appears to accept an unjust society, his 'unmistakeable assault on the order of the family', his even harsher saying to his mother 'Woman, what have we in common?', and the total impracticality of Jesus' advice on matters to do with 'industrial and commercial and economic order' such as his ban on laying up treasure or of taking thought for the morrow (Mt. 6: 19–25). Barth believes that 'there could be no sound or solid economy without this laying up and taking thought'.[35] If Barth is right that such attitudes reflect Jesus' apocalyptic expectations, it is really hard to see how God could possibly be disclosed through such a life. One is tempted to ask how does God being present in Christ 'incognito' significantly differ from not being present at all? I leave a response to Barth on these matters for my subsequent chapters on the historical Jesus and on the divinity of Christ. Suffice it for the present to comment that if one shares the view of many contemporary scholars that we can know quite a lot about Jesus, and if we also find his life and teaching admirable, then this may well lead to a more meaningful understanding of how the personality of God might be disclosed through the language of his human life.

For Barth, what matters is the Christ of the Creeds, and in the Creeds the life and teaching of Jesus is covered by a comma. What matters to Barth is not the historical Jesus, but Jesus as preached as the bringer of redemption. We noted in chapter 2 that the doctrine of the atonement had been a key area of theological controversy during the nineteenth century on the grounds of its morality. In Barth's theology such issues are not raised, because he reinterprets the doctrine of the atonement so that from first to last it is an activity of the triune God:

> It is the eternal God Himself who has given Himself in his Son to be man, and as man to take upon Himself this human passion. His mission: it is the Judge who in this passion takes the place of those who ought to be judged, who in this passion allows Himself to be judged in their place ... He gives Himself to be the humanly acting and suffering person ... It is a matter of the humiliation and dishonouring of God Himself ... In this passion there is legally re-established the covenant between God and man, broken by man but kept by God.[36]

Almost all modern Christians who still talk about the atonement agree with Barth on this. Certainly all the Evangelical contributors to a recent symposium on 'Atonement Today' were unanimous in rejecting older views of the atonement either in terms of a ransom paid to the Devil as in the earlier theologies, or as the Son appeasing or propitiating the wrath of God the Father in later theologies.[37] But there is a real problem in making any kind of sense out of Barth's theory. What is the point of God suffering in Christ in this schema? How does this suffering 're-establish' a covenant between God and man? According to the exemplarist theories of the atonement embraced by the Modernists, Jesus' faithfulness to the death can be understood subjectively as an inspiration to us in the way the deaths of martyrs often are. But Barth wants to keep an objective sense of the atonement as something of absolutely vital significance in the work of redemption. However, as the work of the triune God it becomes completely pointless. In Barth's system God was in no way changed by Jesus' death, in which God was fully present. It was only humankind that was changed by it. But this change is not something which historians or anthropologists can document, any more than the supposedly antecedent 'fall' can be verified or falsified. Once again, as in his discussion of the creation, Barth has kept the old theological terminology but sucked all meaning out of the words in so doing. For although Barth talks constantly of the importance of the cross and passion of Christ, in reality nothing was actually effected by it.

By contrast, although the older objective theories of the atonement were morally appalling and cannot be resurrected today, they did contain good news for those who accepted them. For the early Christians who believed that the human nature of the dying Jesus had been like the bait placed on a fish-hook (St Gregory of Nyssa) or in a mouse-trap (St Augustine) in order to deceive the Devil into swallowing Christ's divinity, which could then destroy the Devil's power, it would be very good news to know that this had happened. Likewise, if one had believed with St Thomas Aquinas, Luther or Calvin that the death of Jesus had been 'a sacrifice by which God was placated', then once again it would have been good news to know that this propitiation had been achieved and God's wrath averted.[38] There was a very powerful message in the much-loved Good Friday hymn:

> He died that we might be forgiven
> He died to make us good,
> That we might go at last to heaven,
> Saved by His precious blood.

There is a lesser but still intelligible sense in the Modernist picture of the exemplary power of Jesus' faithfulness. But there is no good news at all in a death which achieved nothing, even if one could believe that the triune God was present in that death.

This might seem an unfair judgement on Barth, because his interpretation of the redeeming work of Christ seems at first sight to be extended far wider than in the earlier tradition from which he came. Barth rejects Calvin's view that only the 'elect' will be saved, and instead talks of an 'all-inclusive election'. The implication of this is that all will ultimately be saved. This is further implied by Barth's statement that 'God stoops down to the level of us all, both believers and unbelievers ... And it is only by the fact that he knows this, that the believing man is distinguished from the unbeliever.'[39] Once again, this is a change of doctrine which I strongly welcome. Modernism is essentially universalist. But the puzzle remains as to how one can give meaning to Barth's concept of election to eternal life if one cannot give content to this concept. Yet in relation to eternal life, just as in relation to every other of Barth's theological concepts, we find the *appearance* of positive new interpretation, but the *reality* of all content being drained from it.

To the ordinary reader it will seem that Barth is a universalist who speaks of resurrection to eternal life and believes in the resurrection of the body and the life of the world to come. Such is the most natural reading of Barth's many pronouncements in this area, especially in his exposition of the resurrection hope in his book *The Faith of the Church*.[40] For many years I took such language at face value and assumed that Barth believed in a future life. Only through reading Colleen McDannell and Bernhard Lang's book, *Heaven: A History,* and discussing with Lang his own correspondence with Barth did I realize that in talking of the resurrection Barth uses theological language in an exclusively Christological sense. According to Barth, in Jesus Christ we are already in heaven.[41] But as human beings we have no future life to look forward to. We have just one life, which begins at birth and ends at death. This is our 'real and only life'; there can be 'no question of a continuation into an indefinite future of a somewhat altered life'.[42] Resurrection of the body does not mean for Barth what it meant to the early Fathers, that we would rise again to a glorious life in heaven. Rather, it simply means that death will make our lives complete in God.

The paradox of Barth's theology is that so often it sounds utterly orthodox. Bonhoeffer once accused him of presenting a 'positivist doctrine of revelation which says in effect, "like it or lump it": virgin birth, Trinity, or anything else; each is an equally significant and necessary part of the whole, which must simply be swallowed as a whole or not at all'.[43] Bonhoeffer saw Barth's work as 'essentially a restoration' of the traditional position and many other commentators have taken this position.[44] Certainly there are many passages in Barth which encourage this view. For example, in his *Evangelical Theology* he says:

> The theologian will do well not hurriedly [to] ... pass over to demythologising procedures when he is confronted ... by affirmations concerning Jesus' birth from a virgin, and his descent into hell, or by the resurrection of the flesh and the report of the empty tomb, or by the Trinitarian dogmas of Nicea and the Christological dogma of Chalcedon. The theologian might instead ask himself whether he really believes ... in the God of the Gospel when he thinks he can overlook, delete, or reinterpret these and similar points.[45]

However, as we have seen, in reality Barth was not a conservative thinker at all. If one goes beneath the rhetoric of his traditional-sounding religious language to what he really believes, one discovers to one's amazement that little of historic Christianity actually remains. This ought to have become apparent immediately after Barth's death by the fact that Thomas Altizer and William Hamilton, who developed the 'Death of God' theology in the 1960s, described their position as having been 'initiated by Karl Barth and Neo-orthodoxy'.[46] It is similarly relevant that Paul van Buren believed that his own non-cognitive approach to theology leading to a wholly secular understanding of Christianity was the natural consequence of accepting Barth's repudiation of Natural Theology.[47] For if what we mean by the word 'God' is identified exclusively with what we claim to know of Jesus Christ, then we may certainly sound orthodox, and even think of ourselves as orthodox; yet that supposed orthodoxy has been emptied from within of all content. Christomonism and atheism may appear to be at opposite ends of the theological spectrum, but in the final analysis they turn out to be indistinguishable.

4

Modernism in relation to radical and non-realist theologies

For many people Modernist theology is simply part of a continuum of thought from the Enlightenment to the present in
which Christian thinkers have found themselves increasingly
forced to abandon or radically to reinterpret the claims of historical Christianity. Just as the Modernists succeeded the Broad
Churchmen and the liberal Protestants, so they themselves have
been superseded by the more radical existentialist theologies of
Bultmann or Tillich, by Bonhoeffer's non-religious interpretation
of Christianity, the 'Death of God' theology and the secular
meaning of the Gospel, by the political thought of the liberation
theologians, and finally by the explicitly post-Modern theologies
of the 1990s and the Sea of Faith movement, with its wholly non-
realist interpretation of the Christian message. As far as the
history of thought is concerned, there is much to be said for such
a position. This would be supported by the consideration that
since the Second World War the Modern Churchpeople's Union
itself, in its conferences and in its publications, has been
hospitable to the more radical trends of contemporary theology,
leaving behind the fairly well-defined complex of beliefs that
characterized the MCU in the inter-war years.

It is easy to see why the Sea of Faith movement today might
seem the natural end of the process initiated by earlier movements. Compared with their ancestors in the faith, almost all
contemporary Christians are to a greater or lesser extent
non-realist in their understanding of at least some elements in
Christian doctrine. For example, a Christian speaking of the
divine inspiration of the Bible will not usually claim that God
literally dictated the text to the human scribe. Nor are Christians
usually happy to spell out any clear or coherent presentation of
how God can be thought of as acting in history, or providentially

determining what happens to each one of us. Modernists have strenuously criticized the notion that Christ's death literally enables us to become at one with God (at-one-ment) by changing God's attitude to the human race, and even among conservative thinkers few can be found to defend a full-blooded account of hell or judgement. It was characteristic of Modernists to remove any biological content to the concept of the Virgin Birth and to reject the view that Jesus' resurrection entailed the emptiness of his tomb. In the light of this, it might seem entirely reasonable for Bultmann to question whether there was any historical content to belief in the resurrection of Jesus, or for Tillich to question the transcendence of God, or for Bonhoeffer to wonder about the value of religion. When today Don Cupitt and his followers suggest that Christians should take leave of any notion of an objective God, they might seem simply to be taking the final steps along a road which many Christians have been walking.

However, there is a significant difference between the classic Modernist position and the position of the more radical movements of thought which have generally succeeded it. Liberal Protestants and Modernists always claimed to be liberating the kernel of true faith from the husk of outmoded thought. But there is a difference between pruning over-luxuriant growth and pulling up all the flowers by the roots. Liberal Protestants and Modernists characteristically affirmed all the old beliefs, but suggested they be re-interpreted in the light of modern knowledge. Thus, for example, belief in a six-day creation in the relatively recent past was abandoned in favour of belief in God creating through evolution over long periods of time; a degree Christology replaced an ontological Christology; and exemplarist theories of the atonement replaced objective ones. But in all cases the heart of the belief-system was thought to have remained in place. This is not the case with the more radical developments, which suggested very far-reaching changes to the structure of central Christian beliefs.

Let me start with Bultmann's programme for de-mythologizing the Christian message. At first sight he seems to be doing something of which any Modernist would approve. He spells out how much of the language of the New Testament presupposes a myth-ical world-view which is no longer credible. This includes belief in a 'three-decker universe', with heaven in the sky above, earth beneath and an underworld beneath our feet. It also includes belief in angels, evil spirits, miracles and astral forces. It takes for granted literal belief in the fall of Adam, redemption through Christ's blood, and an expectation that Christ will return as judge in the immediate future. For Bultmann none of this can be accepted as true: 'It is simply the cosmology of a pre-scientific age.'[1] Instead, however, of proceeding in the style of a Modernist to the elimination of all this mythology in order to focus on what the historical Jesus taught about God and to explore what can reasonably be believed about his resurrection, Bultmann dismisses these concerns as irrelevant. He thinks it both impossible and unnecessary for faith today to recover the teaching of the historical Jesus, and he makes little attempt to address the question of what it was that gave rise to the resurrection faith of the earliest disciples. According to Bultmann, to address the question of the historicity of the Easter event is not a realistic option: 'An historical fact which involves a resurrection from the dead is utterly inconceivable.'[2] Instead, Bultmann argues that the cross of Jesus, understood as a redemption myth, is the central message (*kerygma*) of the New Testament, and it is on this 'eschatological event' that we must focus. It is this that is the myth that needs to be 'de-mythologized' – not by subtracting it from the Christian message, but by seeking to find its existential significance for us.

Bultmann took for granted the Barthian view that Christ 'meets us in the word of preaching and nowhere else'. Hence he believed that the existential significance of the cross and resurrection of Jesus is shown in the response of Christians to the proclamation of these events. He claims that 'the cross is an ever-present reality in the everyday life of Christians . . . who have crucified the flesh with the passions and lusts thereof'. They have 'overcome the natural dread of suffering and perfected their detachment from the world'.[3] The resurrection, which is 'an article of faith' rather than 'a mythological event', reveals its meaning in the 'newness of life' enjoyed by Christians: 'once again in everyday life . . . Christians participate in Christ's resurrection'. This shows itself in the fact that they 'enjoy a freedom, albeit a struggling freedom, from sin. They are able to cast off the works of darkness . . . and . . . walk honestly as in the day . . . in the power of Christ's resurrection.'[4]

One problem with accepting Bultmann's position is the legitimacy of supposing that the meaning of the cross and resurrection of Jesus can exhaustively be given in terms of the present experience of Christians. If the arguments I shall use later concerning the meaning of Jesus' resurrection as a historical event are valid, then this position would not arise. But a greater problem arises if we ask what evidence we have to support the view that the preaching of either the cross or the resurrection leads or should lead to the life-changes Bultmann predicates. No Christians known to me have 'overcome their natural dread of suffering', and very few would even think it desirable to 'perfect their detachment from the world' or to 'crucify the flesh'. But perhaps this is because we have learned from Dietrich Bonhoeffer that Christians ought not to detach themselves from the problems of the world, and rather than crucifying the passions of the flesh should rejoice in whatever 'earthly bliss' God sends. As Bonhoeffer says, 'to long for the transcendent when you are in your wife's arms is, to put it mildly, a lack of taste'.[5] Similarly with Bultmann's interpretation of the resurrection: is there any sociological evidence that Christians enjoy 'freedom, albeit a struggling freedom, from sin'? Let us recall that at the time Bultmann was making this claim, the Lutheran Church in Germany was hopelessly compromised by its support for the Nazi regime. The fact that Bultmann as an individual was a courageous opponent does not remove the fact that no historian could regard the majority of German Christians as enjoying 'freedom of sin' in their collaboration with Nazi tyranny. This fact in itself is enough to make a nonsense of the proposed reinterpretation of what talk of the resurrection of Jesus means. I suggest further that the swing away from Barth's theological foundation, the new quest for the historical Jesus, new confidence in the objectivity of the resurrection, and declining interest in existentialist philosophy all combine to undermine Bultmann's position.

Bonhoeffer is a far more interesting theologian, whose *Letters and Papers from Prison,* as well as the heroic example of his life and work, have deeply influenced all subsequent Christian life and thought. Many of the themes covered in Bonhoeffer's writings are of permanent importance. I am thinking here of his critique of 'cheap grace', his understanding of what Christian community should be, his rejoicing in the good things of life and the need to develop a 'this-worldly holiness', – to place Christ at the centre of all life, and not confine him to a religious ghetto. I also believe that Bonhoeffer was right to insist that the Church take seriously the autonomy of human thought in a world come of age, and I admire his discussion of the suffering of God and our need to stand alongside God in our concern for the problems of the world. But what seemed in the 1960s to be Bonhoeffer's most distinctive contribution to theology has simply been discovered to be false. Bonhoeffer had assumed that 'we are moving towards a completely religionless time; people as they are now simply cannot be religious any more'. It seemed clear to Bonhoeffer that the 'religious *a priori*' on which historic Christianity had been built might one day no longer exist and would then 'have to be recognized as a historically conditioned and transient form of human self-expression'.[6] Hence the greatest challenge to the Churches for the future would be how to present a 'religionless Christianity' for the new human situation.

Bonhoeffer's challenge was taken up by a host of writers. It became fashionable to talk of 'the secular meaning of the Gospel' or even of 'the death of God'. Among sociologists, the secularization thesis became increasingly dominant and seemed confirmed by a dramatic increase in the pace of decline in participation in the life of the mainstream Churches. Yet from the beginning of the 1970s onwards the secularization thesis has become increasingly problematic. Grace Davie has shown that 'believing without belonging' is extremely common in British society. She points out that 'the decrease in institutional religion has not destroyed religious belief' and suggests that in fact 'nominal (as opposed to organized) Christianity provides a rich seedbed for alternative versions of the sacred'.[7] Christoph Turcke argues that there has been a religious renaissance over the past twenty-five years which has escaped the notice only of those who measure religious practice by Church attendance and membership numbers. He claims that surveys show that many 'who no longer believe in the Christian God . . . still feel religious . . . New Age religion is thriving and . . . atheists can almost seem survivors of a past era.'[8]

In Eastern Europe the collapse of Communism has led to a dramatic increase in the public recognition of the role of religion throughout the former Soviet bloc. Sixty-seven per cent of Russians now describe themselves as Orthodox, and there has been a threefold increase in the number of Russian churches between 1987 and 1996.[9] In the USA the percentage of people who claim they have never doubted the existence of God has risen from 60 per cent in 1987 to 71 per cent in 1997.[10] In China 'social circumstances have changed dramatically in favour of Christian expansion',[11] while in the Muslim world the resurgence of Islam has been so great that Gilles Kepel talks of *The Revenge of God*.[12]

There is much that is puzzling in such figures, but one thing is at least clear, and that is that Bonhoeffer's diagnosis of the end of religion is at least premature. Paul Tillich seems much more in tune with the real human situation in his conviction of the essential religiosity of humankind. Tillich is totally confident that human beings will always ask fundamental questions about the meaning and purpose of existence which only religion can hope to answer. But while there is much that is creative and illuminating in Tillich's discussion, particularly of the importance of correlating theology to other learning, there is a fundamental problem with Tillich's theology in his equation of God with Being Itself. In the end this implies a pantheistic understanding of reality and if the arguments in the next chapter for the existence of God are valid, then Tillich's denial that existence can be properly predicated of God would have to be false.

I do not propose to discuss the varieties of political theology most notably expressed in the Theology of Liberation. This is because, despite the importance of the social problems which gave birth to these theologies, they all ultimately depend on a Marxist analysis of the human situation. What happened in Eastern Europe between 1989 and 1991 has made clear that in every country in which the Communist experiment has been tried it has failed even to deliver the economic goods which were its *raison d'être*. Hence, although it remains the case that Christians have an obligation to work for social justice and human welfare, the framing of a specific theology of liberation does not appear to be the way to advance this cause. Theology is essentially concerned for the being of God and for God's relationship to humankind. What we believe about God, and in particular what we believe to have been the message spoken by God through the Old Testament prophets and the historical Jesus should certainly affect our ethical judgements, but we need to draw a distinction between the study of Christian ethics and the different, even if related, quest for ultimate truths about the nature of reality.

To claim that one is concerned with truths about the nature of reality raises a difficulty for some people today in that, according to 'post-Modernist' thinkers, we simply have no access to such truths. As John Polkinghorne puts it, post-Modernists claim that all our pictures of reality are simply human constructs which 'derive their meaning not from conformity with the way things are, but from conformity with the way our particular community has chosen to speak about them'.[13] Such a view about human knowledge would render scientific inquiry impossible, which is why post-Modernism is almost entirely a phenomenon of humanities departments. In most cases it is a literary theory about how we should interpret literary texts. It does not normally engage with the issues that the theological Modernism of this book is concerned with. However, there is one very influential area of contemporary theology which has fully accepted the post-Modern ideology, and that is the non-realist theology of Don Cupitt. Graham Ward has shown that Cupitt's own position moved from a radical liberalism to non-realism as a result of his reading of the work of French post-structuralist, post-Modern philosophy.[14] This challenges the fundamental presupposition of this book, that the issues it discusses, such as belief in God or in a future life, are about what is or is not the case rather than about how we use human language. In this I take the same approach as that generally taken by modern scientists and hence agree with Polkinghorne that, in resisting post-Modernism, 'science and religion can make common cause'. In the next chapter I shall try to illustrate the new harmony developing between religion, science and philosophy through the work of scholars like Keith Ward and John Polkinghorne; and the case for theological Modernism against literary-studies-style post-Modernism will largely depend on the validity of those arguments.

However, there is another reason for modern theology to reject post-Modernism, and that is that the non-reality of God implicit in post-Modernist claims is incompatible with accepting the authenticity of religious experiencing in which people claim to be in relationship with the divine. This seems to me to the greatest difficulty for non-realist theology, since it is predicated on the view that 'religious values' can be maintained without postulating the existence of God. Yet the 'religious values' that can be shown to have counted most for the religious believer are precisely those of which a non-realist faith cannot take account.

At the heart of all theistic faith is the belief that through prayer, worship, religious or mystical experience, or vision it is possible to enter into a relationship with God. This belief in a divine encounter is utterly undermined by the claim that such experiences do not have any transcendent source, but arise solely from the subjectivity of the believer. Hence the anonymous author of the Epistle to the Hebrews was expressing an important psychological truth about belief when he said that whoever would draw near to God must believe both that God exists and that he rewards those who seek him.[15] Throughout the centuries, countless deeply religious men and women have been haunted by the fear that their faith might be based on a delusion. Muhammad's first response to his sense of a divine call was a fear that it might be nothing more than the product of his own deranged imagination.[16] Four centuries later, shortly after the completion of his elegant argument for God's existence, St Anselm found himself tortured by the thought that perhaps the all-perfect God of his beautifully constructed thought-system was precisely an intellectual construct, and no more. For Anselm this undercut the whole of his religious life. He found himself unable to sleep, eat, pray or fulfil his duties as prior, such was 'the agony and conflict of his thoughts'.[17] For if God exists in the mind alone, and not in reality also, he cannot be that perfect being who alone can be worthy of human devotion. As we know, Anselm ultimately underwent an overwhelming religious experience which he described thus:

> I have found a fullness of joy that is more than full.
> It is a joy that fills the whole heart, mind and
> soul indeed it fills the whole of a man,
> and yet joy beyond measure remains.[18]

On the basis of this experience, St Anselm was led to what would be, for the believer personally, a legitimate conclusion: 'This *is* so truly that it is not possible to think of it as not existing.'[19] And this fact about what is necessary for the personal faith of the devout believer is not affected by any consideration of whether or not St Anselm's 'ontological argument' is philosophically justified. What can be legitimately claimed is that belief in God's reality is a necessary condition for believing that one has entered into a living relationship with him.

What is significant is that both Muhammad and Anselm took for granted that if their religious experience had been auto-induced, and not inspired by a transcendent source, it would thereby have been falsified. Hitherto this has been the all but unanimous view of all Jews, Christians and Muslims, as well as of scholars opposed to these traditions. This is why, over the past two centuries, psychological or sociological theories such as those of Feuerbach, Marx and Freud that have offered alternative explanations for religious feelings have been felt to provide the most damaging critiques of religion. I suggest that they remain so, for if one starts from within the Judaeo-Christian tradition, it is clear that the supreme religious value, as summarized by the Torah, is that God be loved with the whole heart, soul, and strength. Jesus endorsed this, adding to it his own contribution 'and with all your mind'.[20] God cannot be truly loved if we believe him to be only a non-real concept of our own creating. Moreover, if we explore what loving God means by reference to the Psalms of the Old Testament or the Epistles of the New, it is clear that it has two components: personal emotional commitment and devotion, and the thought that such devotion will naturally lead to a wish to keep God's commandments.[21] Comparable claims can be made for Islam, and Sikhism, where what is of supreme religious value is the attitude of adoring submission to God and of obedience to his holy will. In all these theistic traditions, as well as in Bhakti Hinduism, loving devotion to, or humble adoration of, God as a transcendent reality is seen as the supreme religious value. And, hence, any account of 'religious values' which ignores these dimensions, ignores aspects which seem to be at the heart of the religious quest of most of the human race.

From the perspective of the one who prays, religious experience cannot be classified as non-real. When prayer is experienced in terms of encounter, of personal relationship or of communion, it cannot, without contradiction, be thought, by the believer, to be subjective. Only a realist understanding of theism can allow for the genuine possibility of this type of religious experiencing, and if this is thought to be of value, then a non-realist understanding of theology cannot be religiously satisfying.

Cupitt recognizes this. Consequently, although he wishes formal modes of worship to continue, he denies that ecstatic, personal or mystical forms of worship have any authentic place in Christianity. He believes that mystical experience is 'pagan rather than Christian', and derives from 'thwarted eroticism'.[22] In fact this kind of religion is no more than 'sublimated and purified eroticism'. Cupitt believes that 'modern anthropomorphic theism, with its demand for a felt relation to a personal God, has become a different religion from the more austere faith of the ancient and medieval periods'. He thinks that modern piety, with its idea of 'an intimate one-to-one rapport with a vividly experienced guiding and loving fatherly presence', is very different from ancient and medieval prayer which 'was relatively formal, distant and highly ritualized'. Hence, Cupitt thinks that the idea of a felt relationship to God, so far from being the essence of faith, is simply a heterodox and modern distortion of it[23] which has gained power in contemporary Christianity for reasons which Freudian psychology can help us to understand. 'Faith in a personal God' is, for Cupitt, a 'state of erotic fixation or enslavement' from which we need deliverance.[24]

At this point the issue hinges on what one believes is important in the Christian religion. If one accepts a basically Freudian explanation of the theistic religious experience, and if one also accepts Cupitt's historical judgement that belief in a relationship with a personal God represents a modern deviation from authentic Christian spirituality, then the fact that this kind of piety would not be available to a person who accepted non-realism is of no significance. On the other hand, if one thinks that not all mystical experience can be categorized as 'sublimated eroticism', and that many mature and happily married Christians have a strong sense of communion with God, and if one thinks that from the Psalmists onwards a personal relationship with God has been part and parcel of the Judaeo-Christian tradition, then one would come to a very different conclusion. My own reading of the historical data is that the prophets and psalmists in ancient Israel had a very profound sense of closeness to God, and that this understanding was greatly developed in New Testament Christianity. Within the historic tradition I would see the *Confessions* of St Augustine, the writings of the Cappadocian Fathers, the prayers of St Anselm, the hymns of St Bernard, and the poems of the medieval mystics of England as testifying through the ages to the experience of intimate, immediate and close relationship with God as the living heart and fount of Christian spirituality.[25] Hence, I would argue that theological realism is a religious necessity.

It might be thought that I am inconsistent in appealing to Christian experience through the ages to justify a realist position concerning the Christian understanding of God. Yet in chapter 2 I did not hesitate to reject pre-modern understandings in other areas of Christian doctrine. If I believe that the doctrinal systems of people such as St Augustine or St Anselm are now outmoded, why should I be concerned to identify with them when it comes to religious experiencing? I do so because, as Schleiermacher argued in his speeches *On Religion,* what matters most is not the doctrinal systems of the human intellect, which always relate to the world-view of the author's own age, but, rather, the consciousness of the eternal which is the living heart of religious feeling, and which endures across the centuries.[26] The Modernist tradition always sought to separate the kernel from the husk, and part of that kernel was always the awareness of God. In relation to St Augustine and St Anselm, one cannot study their doctrinal works, such as the *Enchiridion* or the *Cur Deus Homo,* without being conscious of the enormous gulf which lies between their understanding of the faith and that of any twentieth-century person. On the other hand, one can read the personal accounts of their relationship with God as set out in St Augustine's *Confessions* and in the *Prayers and Meditations* of St Anselm and feel a sense of fellow-feeling across the centuries. But this sense of God which can be shared with them can only ultimately be valid if a realistic understanding of God is true.

It is therefore not at all surprising that Don Cupitt rejects the validity of personal and mystical prayer and seeks only to defend the kind of formal and liturgical worship in which he continues to feel at home in his Cambridge college chapel. But I fail to see why he feels that participation in such worship is sensible for a person with a non-realist faith. He makes a reasoned case for believing that worship could be justified for both an atheist and a non-realist Christian for the effect it could have on the inwardness of the worshipper, and he believes that, since 'the aim of worship is to declare one's complete and disinterested commitment to religious values',[27] there is no need to postulate the existence of a divine being to validate such worship. His discussion is in many ways reminiscent of Kant's justification for worship in his *Religion within the Limits of Reason Alone*. Kant believed that godliness should 'merely serve as a means of strengthening that which in itself goes to make a better man, to wit, the virtuous disposition', and consequently that the only authentic purpose of prayer or worship is to establish goodness in ourselves and to spread abroad such goodness within the ethical community. However, Kant recognized that this was all completely theoretical, since the worship actually on offer in the Christian Churches was inappropriate for the purposes he had in mind, and indeed unhelpful to them. Hence, he never actually attended public worship, and even made a point of leaving university processions at the church door.[28]

The point is that worship in all the Christian Churches is thoroughly realist and, under the influence of the ecumenical and liturgical movements, is becoming more and more uniform, focusing on the Eucharist and therein rehearsing a constant succession of propositional claims about God and his saving activity in the life and work of Christ. Liberal Christians often find their worshipping marred by the pre-critical way these claims are presented, but by a process of internal reinterpretation they are enabled to continue in their participation. For liberals characteristically believe themselves not to be abandoning, but to be reappropriating, essential truths contained in outmoded forms. It is much harder to see why a non-realist should worship, because for the non-realist there is no inner core of truth to be discovered.

Cupitt has sought to meet this objection by pointing out that much of Christian worship consists of Old Testament material which reflects a religion, society and culture utterly removed from the thought-world of the contemporary Christian.[29] If for two thousand years Christians have used in their worship the hymn-book of the second Jewish Temple without endorsing the belief-system assumed by it, why cannot the contemporary non-realist celebrate a Christian Eucharist with just as much ease? But this analogy will not do. Christians have not used the Old Testament in its own right. In pre-critical days a tradition of reinterpretation led the Old Testament to be read through Christian spectacles and reinterpreted to illustrate Christian themes. Since the rise of criticism the Old Testament has been less and less used and, at least in the main Sunday worship, only such carefully selected extracts as accord with Christian ideals continue to be read. In particular, the Psalms have been used, not as alien literature, but because they articulate what Christians wish to say. Hence, I reject the analogy and suggest that only for a realist faith does Christian worship remain a sensible activity. It should be noted that the arguments I have hitherto used in associating worship with realism apply even more strongly in other religious contexts. Since celibacy is regarded as sinful in Zoroastrianism, and is not valued in Islam, Freudian interpretations of their worship are much less plausible. In the case of Islamic worship the prayer is wholly centred on the adoration and praise of God and would become a nonsensical activity if God were thought to be unreal. The same also applies to Sikhism and to Hindu worship in the Bhakti tradition.

It might be thought that I have laid too much weight on religious 'feeling'. I have done so because the possibility of a personal relationship with God is of crucial importance to a realist account of faith today. The strength of the non-realist case is that many professed theists have an entirely secular world-view, in that their expectations of life are not affected by their belief in God. For most Christians, belief in particular providence perished with the rise of actuarial statistics, the indiscriminate slaughter of the First World War, and the holocaust of European Jewry in the Second. And though some may continue to believe in special divine intervention or answered prayer, the problems of fitting alleged instances into any coherent theodicy seem insuperable. So the question arises in a starkly clear form: 'What difference does belief in God make?' Unless some answer can be given to this question, the non-realist case is established. Only two answers seem possible: first, that, through the existence of a personal relationship with God, the human situation can be transformed from within; second, that, in the light of the quality of the personal relationship with God, it may seem for the believer plausible to hope that God will wish to sustain the relationship through death. Are these answers intelligible?

At least some believers do claim that their consciousness of God's presence has utterly transformed otherwise intolerable situations. Bishop Leonard Wilson of Birmingham, who ordained me, affirmed that he had never been so conscious of God's sustaining and redeeming love than when he was being tortured in Changi prisoner-of-war camp. In external terms God did precisely nothing. No particular providence rescued him from his torturers, and yet his sense of the presence of God suffering with him in his distress not merely transformed the situation for him then, but subsequently sustained him in his faith for the rest of his life.[30] This is no isolated case but is typical of the record of countless Christian martyrs and sufferers through the ages. Now of course there are problems with such claims. No doubt a psychological theory of compensatory projection can be constructed, and cases can be raised, as in the instance of Jesus' cry of dereliction from the cross, when God seems wholly to abandon the sufferer at precisely the time when he is most needed. Nevertheless, it is significant that belief in divine grace can make a difference to human experience of events in the world, both in some cases of suffering and through conversion experiences. It may be impossible to demonstrate to others that such experiences arise from anything other than the human subconscious. But it is essential for the believer to suppose that they come from a transcendent source. The experience has its transforming power because it is believed to come from a real God.

Belief in a life after death is another case where a difference between realist and non-realist interpretations of faith becomes apparent. For Christians who interpret life after death as a factual claim, belief stems from their trust in the constancy of God, his power and his love. I believe it can be shown that, throughout the history of Christian thought, belief in a future life has been of supreme importance, that it has been understood in a thoroughly realist sense and that it has significantly affected the way Christians have looked at life.

Cupitt, however, believes that 'it is spiritually important that one should not believe in life after death but should instead strive to attain the goal of the spiritual life in history'.[31] He believes that faith in a future life should be rejected on religious grounds because it conflicts with his understanding of disinterestedness as the supreme spiritual value. To love God for the sake of benefits, whether in this life or the next, would be spiritually corrupting. Hence, in prayer we should learn to expect no benefits, whether earthly or heavenly, but follow St John of the Cross in the purgative way through the ascent of Mount Carmel.[32] In this context Cupitt (but not St John of the Cross!) believes that 'it is a great help to be a religious person who does not believe in life after death'. For realizing the finality of our death helps to liberate us from self-concern. Hence we should reject realist claims about a future life on religious grounds – quite apart from the fact that there is 'no chance' of them being realized since we are 'quite certain to die and be annihilated'.[33]

On one point I fully agree with Cupitt: virtue is its own reward and ought to be embraced for its own sake irrespective of any notion of subsequent reward or punishment in a future life. On the key point at issue, however, I think that a Christian realist must question Cupitt's interpretation of disinterestedness as an absolute value. The doctrine is not biblical, but entered Christian thought from Cicero's work *On Friendship*. Peter Abelard was the first Christian writer to argue that our love for God should be wholly disinterested, and Etienne Gilson has shown that Abelard came to this view, not simply from reading Cicero, but because he felt that the selfless and enduring love of Heloise for him throughout the calamities of his life represented the highest form of human love.[34] Though I would agree that Heloise's fidelity was indeed commendable, it would seem better for all concerned when love is able to be mutually fulfilling. And though God should be loved simply because he is love, I do not think Abelard was being necessarily inconsistent when he also looked forward to the joys of heaven in his great hymn O *quanta qualia*. To love God for the sake of heaven would indeed be akin to using friendship as a means of place-seeking. But to find joy in religious experience and to look forward to the beatific vision is not a distortion but a fulfilment of what a relationship with God can be. As Austin Farrer put it: 'Heaven is not a payment for walking with God; it's where the road goes.'[35]

It is not surprising that Cupitt should highlight those elements in earlier Christian tradition that have spoken of the unknowability of God, of the importance of a disinterested approach to him, and of the Dark Night of the Soul, in which prayer seems to go dead. He sees a non-realist account of theology as the natural successor to such teachings. And it is indeed true that many of the greatest thinkers of the Christian past would have been dismayed by the confident anthropomorphism of much contemporary preaching, and the auto-induced religious euphoria of some charismatic developments. Christian apologetic can be too realist and may present a too easily conceptualized idol in place of the one who transcends all that we can imagine or describe.

Nevertheless, the fact remains that though the greatest Fathers of the Church were conscious of the ambiguity of human language, and of the limitations of human thought, they were in the end theological realists. They believed that in the darkness they had indeed encountered the holy and living God in whom they lived and moved and had their being.[36] Of none was this more true than St John of the Cross. Cupitt encourages his readers and his students to suppose that this great Doctor of the Church arrived at the same concept of the *nihil* as himself.[37] This is profoundly misleading, for, as my colleague Tom O'Loughlin has pointed out to me, Cupitt assumes *nihil* means 'nothingness or void', whereas for St John *nihil* simply meant 'no thing'. The reason why St John wished for no 'thing' was because things can distract us from God our creator. Cupitt failed to understand St John on this issue because he consciously decided to disregard all the saint's poems, which speak at length of 'the sense of God living constantly in the soul, of the warmth of reciprocal love, and of God's goodness in all things' and they clearly emerge from the saint's 'direct and joyful experience of God'.[38] Any similarity between the *via negativa* of the mystical tradition and the non-realism of contemporary Christian philosophy is very much a matter of the surface only and does not extend to the depths of historic faith.

What is valued most in the Christian tradition is a sense of the presence of God. This supreme value is contingently dependent on the believer remaining convinced that God exists in reality as well as in our minds. It may be that our whole culture is passing through a Dark Night of the Soul and that a genuine recovery of faith is a future possibility. This possibility will be realized if, and only if, Christians can defend the objective reality of the being of God.

5

Modern science and the arguments for God's existence

From the outset the Modernist movement in the Church of England was deeply concerned with the relationship between science and religion, and in particular with the absolute necessity for the Church to accept the reality of evolution in its understanding of God's relation to the cosmos. 'The Scientific Approach to Religion' was the theme of MCU conferences in 1924 and 1963 attended by many leading thinkers of the day.[1] F. R. Tennant's *Philosophical Theology,* published in 1928, contained a defence of the argument from design which in many respects foreshadowed much of today's thinking; and other Modernists, such as Charles Raven and W. R. Matthews, constantly urged the relevance of Natural Theology to the coherence of Christian belief. In spite of their best efforts, the subject was largely disregarded within the Christian Churches. At the beginning of the 1960s Ninian Smart described Natural Theology as the 'the sick man of Europe' and lamented that many theologians seemed unconcerned about this. Howard Root followed this up: in his contribution to *Soundings* in 1964, he argued for the recovery of Natural Theology as vital to any theology which is to engage with the contemporary world.[2]

It is thus noteworthy that in the 1990s a new interest in Natural Theology has come to the fore among a number of scientists and philosophers of religion. This has focused on the relevance of recent developments in physics to two of the classic arguments for the existence of God. The reason for this interest is that there appears to be a surprising correlation between what scientists have discovered about the universe and what the theistic religions have historically claimed. Judaism, Christianity and Islam affirm that the universe and time were created from nothing by God. They also affirm that the universe is God's handiwork in the sense that God designed all that is. Science as such can make no comment on claims of this sort. As Kant argued in his *Critique of Pure Reason,* science can only work within the limits of what is ultimately available to us through the senses as interpreted within the categories of space and time. Since God cannot be known through the senses and transcends both space and time, his reality is not of the kind that science can make any comment upon. On the other hand, if science were to conclude that the universe did come into being literally from nothing, and if the fundamental constants of the universe gave the appearance of having been 'carefully chosen' with a view to the evolution of 'observers', then such conclusions would at least be highly congruent with the concept of a creative mind behind the cosmos. Let us explore the evidence behind such notions.

The first phenomenon I want to look at is the hypothesis usually referred to as the 'Big Bang' theory of creation. This is the claim that the universe as we know it has not always existed but came into being from nothing 15 billion years ago. Four leading astronomers put it like this: 'The universe began with a great explosion from a state of infinite density about 15 billion years ago ... space and time were created in that event and so was all the matter in the universe.'[3] But, as William Craig points out, 'infinite density' is precisely equivalent to 'nothing'. No object can possess infinite density, for 'if it had any size at all it would not be infinitely dense'.[4] Hence, a literal application of the Big Bang model implies that the universe came into existence from 'nothing at all'. There is a strong consensus among contemporary scientists, including Russian scientists, that this is so.[5]

No consequences necessarily follow from accepting this fact. From a strictly scientific perspective, one can simply accept as an ultimate fact about reality that the universe came into existence from nothing 15 billion years ago. Antony Flew defends this view strongly, reminding us that well over 2,000 years ago Straton of Lampsacus had contended that 'the existence of the universe and whatever may be discovered to be its fundamental laws ought simply to be accepted as the explanatory ultimates for which no further explanation is either necessary or possible'. From Flew's perspective, Stratonician atheism is therefore as valid as ever, and he calls for scientists such as Stephen Hawking to cease talking about the 'the Mind of God' as if this could provide some 'other kind of cause'.[6] Flew's view is similar to that of Peter Atkins, who insists that that 'the whole universe tumbled out of absolutely nothing' but adds: 'There is no purpose behind it, it just happened to happen.'[7]

Other scientists are less happy about such a view. As Stephen Hawking says in his *Black Holes and Baby Universes*, after everything that science can say, 'You still have the question: why does the universe bother to exist? If you like, you can define God to be the answer to that question.'[8] Clearly, such a response is not the only one. It remains possible that the sudden emergence of the universe, and the surprising way it developed, will always remain inexplicable. But from a scientific point of view there is something very odd about Atkins's claim that it 'just happened to happen'. The whole scientific enterprise got under way only when people stopped supposing that things just happened to happen and began to look for explanations, reasons and causes. Certainly within the natural order this is utterly axiomatic, so it is puzzling when it comes to the cosmos as a whole that one should abandon the quest for explanation. The problem is, of course, that if one is to give any kind of explanation for the whole cosmos tumbling out of absolutely nothing, one is forced to posit some cause which transcends the cosmos, and this is a very challenging concept.

In fact the reason why the 'Big Bang' is thought by many physicists to be relevant to belief in God is that it appears to give an empirical foundation for an important version of the cosmological argument for God's existence. This is known as the Kalam Cosmological Argument and was developed by two medieval Islamic scholars, Al-Kindi and Al-Ghazali. It goes like this:

1. Everything that begins to exist has a cause of its existence.
2. The universe began to exist.
3. Therefore the universe has a cause of its existence.[9]

Philosophers have always accepted that if the first two premisses were true, the conclusion would follow. But during the Middle Ages the second premiss was derived from a complicated and to us not very convincing philosophical argument about the logical impossibility of an actually infinite temporal series, so the argument did not carry much weight and is generally thought to have been refuted by Kant in his first *Critique*. What Kant argued is that any alleged proof 'attempted independently of empirical principles' and simply asserting the impossibility of infinite regress on speculative principles of reason in fact presupposes what it seeks to establish and is therefore subject to all the objections he had earlier raised against the ontological argument.[10] Richard Swinburne fully agrees that there is no future in *a priori* arguments which purport to show that the universe must have had a beginning. But the whole situation is transformed if the argument is based on *a posteriori* observation by scientists that as a matter of empirical fact the universe did have a beginning.[11] Once this is accepted, the second premiss seems to be true.

That leaves the first premiss: 'everything that begins to exist has a cause of its existence'. Here I have to confess that I share William Craig's view that this premiss is 'so intuitively obvious ... that probably no one in his right mind *really* believes it to be false. Even David Hume himself confessed that his academic denial of the principle's demonstrability could not eradicate his belief that it was none the less true.'[12] What Hume actually wrote was: 'Allow me to tell you that I never asserted so absurd a proposition as *that anything might arise without a cause*: I only maintained that our Certainty of the Falsehood of that Proposition proceeded neither from Intuition nor Demonstration; but from another Source.'[13]

All that Hume had intended to show was that the principle of causation was not analytic, and therefore it was *logically* possible that it *might* not always apply. However, all our experience teaches us that in real life the principle of causation in fact *always does apply*. As Craig says: 'Constantly verified and never falsified, the causal proposition may be taken as an empirical generalisation enjoying the strongest support experience affords.'[14] It is therefore not unreasonable to suppose that the principle of causation, which applies to everything of which we have experience, should also apply to the universe itself. And if we accept that the universe came into being from nothing, it is rational to postulate a transcendent cause of its existence.

Flew points out that all the argument actually establishes is the existence of a 'physically unknowable cause of the Big Bang'.[15] Yet this is a by no means insubstantial thing to have established, and it is certainly far more than Flew would have conceded as possible before the rise of the new cosmology. Ninian Smart suggests that the argument shows the existence of a 'Cosmos-Explaining-Being' and argues that, to be religiously important, the idea would have to be enriched.[16] This is undoubtedly true. The God of the religious believer is *more* than the 'physically unknowable cause of the Big Bang' being postulated by this argument. But God is *not less* than the creator. It is no accident that all the Christian Creeds start with affirming belief in the Creator. They then go on to affirm that this creator has made himself known in Christ. But the starting-point is belief in God. Similarly in Jewish and Islamic thought: what matters for Judaism is the covenant between God and Israel, and what matters for Islam is the belief that Muhammad was the definitive prophet of God through whose recitation of the Qur'ān, God's will has been made known. But in all cases the initial belief in God is the necessary condition for further beliefs about God's character and his mode of self-disclosure.

In this argument the concept of God being employed is either the timeless God of classic theism or the biblical picture of God as 'from everlasting to everlasting'.[17] In neither case does it make sense to ask 'What caused God?' The first premiss of the Kalam Cosmological Argument is that 'anything that begins to exist has a cause of its existence'. Since no theist believes that God began to exist, that question has no application to God.

The coming into being of everything from nothing does not compel belief in God, because, as we have already noted, it is always open to an atheist to say that if the universe did come into being from nothing this should simply be regarded as an inexplicable fact. But one can at least legitimately say that the widespread belief among modern physicists that the universe exploded into existence from nothing at all is more compatible with the theistic belief that God created the universe out of nothing than any previous secular scientific world-view, and this is a highly significant development.

However, although there is a strong consensus that the universe as we know it began with the Big Bang, a significant number of physicists deny that this should be understood as an absolute beginning. Some believe that, provided enough matter exists in the universe, there will come a time when gravitational forces will eventually stop the expansion of the universe and it will collapse on itself in a 'Big Crunch' analogous to the Big Bang. If this will happen in the distant future, then it is likely that it also happened in the distant past and, hence, that the Big Bang was the ultimate product of an earlier Big Crunch! Another theory is the quantum fluctuation theory. This holds that it was only matter that originated in the Big Bang, but that background space–time, quantum field and laws of nature were already in operation.[18] A third theory is the Hartle–Hawking model. According to Ward, this seeks 'to eliminate the background space–time and generates the temporal state of this universe out of a wider timeless domain of three-spaces linked in "fuzzy" ways. The model aims to resolve time as we experience it into a wider mathematically statable reality.'[19] The key point in this theory is that it presupposes that the universe has no beginning or end, no boundary or edge. Hawking believes that if this theory were to be confirmed it would raise in an acute form the question 'What place then for a Creator?'[20] On the other hand, as we shall see, Hawking is quite clear that the Big Bang plays a key role in the way our current universe has developed and that the fundamental constants of reality are extremely finely tuned; and this might point in a rather different direction. If any of these alternative theories to the classic Big Bang view end up by gaining general acceptance, then the Kalam Cosmological Argument would need to be modified. It would lose its original primary premiss, which was that the universe literally began from nothing and hence requires a transcendent cause to explain its coming into being. One would have to argue instead that the state of the universe before and after the Big Bang was so fundamentally different that the coming into being of this fundamentally different universe requires a transcendent cause. We shall return to this issue later when we see how great these differences actually are. But before doing so we might note that if the universe in some sense always existed as posited both by a theory of oscillation between Big Crunch and Big Bang and also by the Hawking–Hartle model, this would pose no difficulty for the traditional understanding of the cosmological argument.

Christian theological tradition has for the most part accepted the assumption of St Thomas Aquinas that the dependence of the universe upon God has nothing whatever to do with whether or not the universe began to exist or not. The same conclusion was reached by Muslim philosophers such as Ibn Sina (Avicenna) or

Ibn Rushd (Averroes) who did not work within the Kalam framework of Al Ghazali.[21] Both Aquinas and his Muslim counterparts thought that belief in creation *ex nihilo* was a doctrine derived from scripture rather than philosophy. From a philosophical point of view, even if the universe had existed from all eternity it would still be dependent on God.

Keith Ward is a strong contemporary defender of this view. He argues that the 'intelligibility, beauty and (mathematical) harmony of the universe',[22] as described by modern mathematical physics, might best be interpreted as showing 'how the material cosmos can be understood as arising from a deeper, intelligible, beautiful and non-material reality. This paves the way for a better understanding of God as a self-existent reality which generates the whole material universe.'[23] He thinks that there are many far more cogent reasons for believing in God than just positing his existence to account for a supposed 'first temporal moment'. Indeed, Ward believes that the nature of the existence of the universe is a far more compelling reason for believing in God than the coming into existence of the universe would be. For Ward it would be odder to suppose that the universe as a 'highly ordered mathematical domain exists on its own than to say that a material universe just comes into being on its own'.[24]

This understanding of the cosmological argument leads very naturally to a consideration of the second new argument for the existence of God: namely, the argument derived from 'the fine-tuning of the universe'. The starting-point is that 'Cosmologists, physicists and astronomers have identified a number of special conditions which had to be fulfilled in the structure and evolution of the universe if human life was one day to exist within it.'[25] These conditions, often referred to as 'cosmic coincidences', have led to the formulation of the so-called 'anthropic principle', which suggests that the way the universe came into being and subsequently evolved was in some way related to the emergence of human life. This principle is based on the discovery over the past twenty to thirty years of

> how complex and sensitive a nexus of conditions must be given in order for the universe to permit the origin and evolution of intelligent life on earth. Today in the various fields of physics, astrophysics, classical cosmology, quantum mechanics and

biochemistry, various discoveries have repeatedly disclosed that the existence of intelligent carbon-based life on earth at this time depends upon a delicate balance of physical and cosmological constants such that were any of these quantities to be slightly altered the balance would be destroyed and life would not exist.[26]

Such facts almost instinctively lead one in the direction of thinking about God. As Hawking observes in his *Brief History of Time:* 'The initial state of the universe must have been very carefully chosen indeed if the hot big bang model was correct right back to the beginning of time. It would be very difficult to explain why the universe should have begun this way, except as the act of a God who intended to create beings like us.'[27]

When Hawking says that the initial state of the universe must have been 'very carefully chosen' he refers to what writers describe as the 'fine-tuning' of the universe in the first moments of creation. For example, Hawking says that the heat of the universe one second after the Big Bang had to be exactly as it was because a decrease of heat by as little as one part in a million million would have caused the universe to collapse. One part in a million million is 10^{12}, a fantastically remote chance. But other features of the universe had to be even more 'carefully chosen': electromagnetism and gravity had to be correct to one part in 10^{40}, the rate of expansion to 10^{55}, density to 10^{60} and the smoothness of expansion to 10^{123}. All these and many other constants had to come right simultaneously for the universe to come into being and to evolve in the way it did. Paul Davies says that the odds against all of them coming right together are at least one followed by a thousand billion, billion zeros. The evidence cited above is derived from the work of leading mathematical physicists as summarized in John Leslie's acclaimed work *Universes.*[28] For anyone who is not a mathematician it is difficult to understand the basis on which the authorities cited by Leslie work out these figures. However, it seems that the fact of the fine-tuning of the universe seems to be agreed by all concerned, whichever way they subsequently interpret such facts.

The evidence for the fine-tuning of the universe totally destroys Hume's attempted refutation of the argument from design by postulating instead the Epicurean hypothesis that, given unlimited time, the particles of the universe would go through every combination possible to them. For we simply do not have unlimited time available; moreover, the statistical chances relating to the fine-tuning of the universe are unimaginably greater than the number of sub-atomic particles in the universe.

The question is how one explains the fact that if up to thirty of the most significant physical features of the universe had been infinitesimally different, galaxies would not have formed, planetary systems would not have developed and human beings would never have evolved.[29] The universe looks as if it had been 'designed with the goal of generating and sustaining observers'.[30] This is what lies behind the development and discussion of the so-called 'Anthropic Principle'. This exists in both 'Weak' and 'Strong' forms. The Weak Anthropic Principle says: 'We must be prepared to take account of the fact that our location in the universe is necessarily privileged to the extent of being compatible with our existence as observers.' However, the chances seem far too remote to be content simply with that position. Let me give an analogy which I have heard Richard Swinburne develop. Imagine a prisoner before a firing squad. All twelve soldiers miss on three occasions and therefore the prisoner is freed. We would not be content to account for his survival simply on the basis that had he not survived the story could not be told. Instead we would look for explanations in terms of the motivation of those who aimed to miss. So too with our presence as observers in the cosmos. The odds are so unlikely that they cry out for explanation in terms of purpose. Hence, to make sense of the cosmos one seems compelled to move to the Strong Anthropic Principle and say: 'The universe (and hence the parameters on which it depends) must be such as to admit the creation of observers within it at some stage.'[31] In other words the fine-tuning of the universe leads most naturally to the view that, as Davies puts it, 'God has designed the Universe so as to permit such life and consciousness to emerge'.[32] Here, 'far from exposing human beings as incidental products of blind physical forces, science suggests that the existence of conscious organisms is a fundamental feature of the universe. We have been written into the laws of nature in a deep, and I believe meaningful way.'[33]

Does this agreed evidence for the fine-tuning of the universe prove the existence of a designer God? Not absolutely, for if there were an infinite number of universes, or even many thousand trillions of universes, one might expect a few to evolve naturally in the way ours has done.[34] Hence H. Everett's 'many-world quantum theory' has developed as a naturalistic way of making sense of the phenomena which others attribute to a designer God.[35]

However, one of the most basic principles of science is 'Ockham's Razor', according to which the simplest hypothesis is always the most plausible, and as a philosopher one should always 'claim existence for as few non-sensible realities as one possibly can' (or, in the traditional Latinized translation, should 'avoid multiplying entities beyond necessity'). In this context one could argue that the many-world quantum theory is the most extreme possible instance of a defiance of Ockham's Razor. To invoke an infinity of universes in order to explain the remarkable features of the only universe of which we have any knowledge is a remarkable alternative to the God hypothesis. As Richard Swinburne comments, 'faced with such difficulties, we could judge it altogether better to reject the many-universes approach, putting our trust instead in the God hypothesis'.[36] The same conclusion is reached by the mathematical physicist turned theologian John Polkinghorne, who argues against the many-world hypothesis: 'a metaphysical suggestion of equal coherence and greater economy is that there is only one universe which is the way it is because it is not any old world, but the creation of a Creator who wills it to be capable of fruitful process'.[37]

Sir Roger Penrose argues that for our universe to come into being in the way it has done the 'Creator's aim' must have been precise to an accuracy of one part in '10 to the 10 to the 123'. Penrose points out that this is such an extraordinary figure that no one could possibly even write the number down in full. If we were to write it out in the ordinary denary notation it would be 1 followed by so many '0's that 'if we were to write an "0" on each separate proton and each separate neutron in the entire universe – and we could throw in all the other particles as well – we should fall short of writing down the figure needed'.[38] When one is talking of odds like this, there seems no meaningful difference between creating out of nothing at all, and selecting at odds of this inconceivable order out of the phase space of possible universes!

The second range of data we explored was all based on the apparent agreement that our universe has been incredibly finely tuned, as if for the purpose of the emergence of life and mind. This can be regarded as a new version of the 'argument from design'. These new arguments from modern science do not prove the existence of God, but they do show that belief in God is a very reasonable way of making sense of the way the world is. Faced with such evidence, belief in God might seem more probable than any alternative explanations of reality. This is a radically different situation from that which applied in the recent past in the intellectual world. But I believe it does show that perhaps believers in God might legitimately claim the high ground in the contemporary debate.

However, the discussion of modern scientific cosmological theories in relation to belief in God shows that a serious problem of communication exists between the worlds of science and of theology. In this chapter I have quoted frequently from the work of Hawking, who frequently talks of God, and who clearly believes in the fine-tuning of the universe. He accepts the possible legitimacy of defining 'God' as the answer to the question why the universe exists, and he thinks that if we could 'discover a complete theory ... then we would know the mind of God'. But Hawking would not regard himself as a Christian or a theist, and he is more often quoted as a critic than as a supporter of theistic belief. In one summary of his beliefs he explained his position as follows: 'physics suggests the possibility of a mathematical God, but not a being with whom one can have a personal relationship, which is what people normally mean by "God".'[39] One is left with the feeling that, while much of his scientific thinking seems to be leading him in the direction of belief in a mind behind the cosmos, he is repelled by the anthropomorphism and triviality of such discussion of God as he has encountered.

Hawking is not at all unusual in this. According to Fred Hoyle, 'While most scientists claim to eschew religion, it actually dominates their thoughts more than it does the clergy.'[40] Hoyle openly acknowledges that his own atheism was shaken by the discovery of the fine-tuning of the universe:

A commonsense interpretation of the facts suggests that a super-intellect has monkeyed with physics, as well as with chemistry and biology, and there are no blind forces worth speaking about in nature. The numbers one calculates from the facts seem to me so overwhelming as to put this conclusion almost beyond question.[41]

Paul Davies's position seems not to be far removed from this. He believes that 'science offers a surer path to God than religion' in that 'science has actually advanced to the point where what were formerly religious questions can be seriously tackled'.[42] But Davies is very critical of the dogmatism of religion and has not aligned himself with any religious tradition.

The tragedy is that, though it appears that many aspects of modern physics are more sympathetic to theism than science has been for centuries, many scientists do not want to associate themselves with contemporary religion, which they experience as simplistic, dogmatic and antagonistic. In Keith Ward's fascinating account of modern science he shows over and over again that, properly understood, the findings of modern scientists most naturally support the theism they are actually criticizing. In particular he shows that Peter Atkins's arguments in *Creation Revisited* 'ought to lead' to a belief 'in the mind of God',[43] just as Hawking's hypothesis 'paves the way for a better understanding of God'.[44] However, the two most significant instances Ward alludes to are those of Steven Weinberg and of John Leslie, for both these thinkers explicitly acknowledge the importance of teleological reasons and a sense of beauty and elegance in choosing ultimate theories. For example, Weinberg comments: 'there is beauty in these laws, that mirrors something that is built into the structure of the universe'. Ward holds that these two thinkers do not believe in God 'because they cannot connect the idea of the ultimate value of beauty with what they (wrongly) see as the very anthropomorphic and rather sentimental God of religion'.[45]

This is particularly true in the case of Leslie, whose book *Universes* has been strongly acclaimed as one of the finest presentations of the argument from design. Leslie makes it very clear that he is not concerned with 'the kind of God who designs the structures of individual organisms, plague germs perhaps, or who interferes with Nature's day to day operations'.[46] Yet Leslie believes that 'our universe does look . . . very much as if created by God'.[47] But the kind of God to which this evidence points is more like the God of Neoplatonism than the God of popular Christianity. Leslie believes that modern science appears to show us that 'if God is real then his reality seems ... most likely to be as described by the Neoplatonist theological tradition'.[48] This, however, should not be regarded as a 'replacement' for the Christian God. 'Neoplatonism's creative principle ... *is* God to a great many Catholic, Protestant and Greek Orthodox thinkers, and many others are at least willing to grant that God may be like this, Neoplatonism has been a strong element in Christian theology since its beginnings.'[49]

From a Modernist perspective it is fascinating to note that what Leslie argues in the light of modern science is precisely what Dean Inge argued sixty years ago on the basis of his study of Plotinus. Dean Inge was president of the MCU in its most influential period from 1924 to 1934 and was forthright in his defence of the Neoplatonist concept of God. He claimed uncompromisingly that Neoplatonism 'is of course the Christian view and I believe it will vindicate itself against the rival view of a Deity who is vitally involved in the life of His creatures'.[50] If God is to be credible to a modern person, then what is claimed about God must be compatible with the rest of what we know about the nature of reality. So much of popular belief about God is far too anthropomorphic to be credible, and a greater austerity in thinking about God would correspond to the wisdom of mystics and saints, who have insisted on how little we can know of God. From a Neoplatonist perspective, God is better thought of as a creative force, than an almighty person, but God is 'personal' in being concerned 'with creating persons and acting as a benevolent person would. To be more specific, Neoplatonism's God is the world's creative ethical requirement.'[51]

Keith Ward is 'not averse to' interpreting the universe as described by mathematical physicists such as Roger Penrose as 'a Platonic world of pure mathematical forms. For a theist, this is indeed quite a natural interpretation for where else would the mathematical forms be but in the mind of God?'[52] He argues that the picture of the universe as 'a highly ordered mathematical domain' fits very well with the 'theistic hypothesis' that 'the material world originates from a more stable and enduring conceptual (or spiritual) realm'. Ward believes that, so far from making God superfluous, Hawking's thought is better understood as showing 'how the material cosmos can be understood as arising from a deeper, intelligible, beautiful and non-material reality'. For though the quasi-Platonic ontology of some mathematical physics does not *require* the postulation of a God, the natural place for conceptual realities to exist is in some supra-cosmic mind. From Philo onwards, Platonists have tended to locate the Forms in a divine mind. And it is not wholly without significance that Hawking speaks, however ironically, of knowing the ultimate laws of nature as 'knowing the mind of God'.[53]

The point that is being argued here is that modern mathematical physics describes a picture of reality which can be shown to be highly compatible with belief in God as creator and sustainer of the universe. This is so whether or not the universe had a beginning literally from nothing, even though a beginning from nothing might make the need for God more readily apparent. It has, however, also been argued that if one does accept that mathematical physics can help us to understand God, this will have an impact on the kind of God in which we believe. For both Ward and Leslie, a Neoplatonist understanding of God very readily accords with the picture given by mathematical physics. But neither of them would agree with Dean Inge that this correlation is so close that 'Christianity and Platonism stand or fall together'.[54] There is a variety of Christian positions compatible with modern science. The one key consideration is that one cannot argue for the existence of God on the basis of the harmony and order displayed in the natural order and simultaneously believe in a God who is constantly intervening in everyday life.

The perspective of the classic Modernists is highly relevant here. For Modernists have always argued that God works through the natural order, not in violation of it. Their view was endorsed as a legitimate perspective in the 1938 report on *Doctrine in the Church of England*. Having noted that some believe that miracle has a special value, the report goes on to say: 'On the other hand it is to be recognised that many others feel it to be more congruous with the wisdom and majesty of God that regularities, such as men of science observe in nature and call Laws of Nature, should serve his purpose without any need for exceptions'.[55] This view, which represented the Modernist position sixty years ago, is even more relevant today. The general view among committed Christian physicists is that, although in theory God might intervene in nature, in practice he does not. This is expressed succinctly by Arthur Peacocke, who writes:

Given that ultimately God is the Creator of the world ... we cannot rule out the possibility that God might 'intervene', in the popular sense of the word, to bring about events for which there can never be a naturalistic interpretation ... But we have ... cogent reasons for questioning whether such direct 'intervention' is normally compatible with and coherent with other well-founded affirmations concerning the nature of God and of God's relation to the world.[56]

Similarly, Polkinghorne, who moved from the chair of Mathematical Physics at Cambridge to ordination to the Anglican priesthood, believes that a theist is 'loath to invoke direct divine intervention (in the world)':[57]

The very last thing that the utterly consistent and rational God can be is a kind of capricious celestial conjuror ... those laws of nature whose regularities are discerned by science are understood by the theologian to be willed by God and to reflect God's continuing faithfulness. God cannot work against the laws of nature for that would be for God to work against himself.[58]

None of this implies that God is unrelated to the world, solely that the mode of God's relationship is through the religious experiences of the believer.

6

Modern confidence in the historical Jesus

Christianity has always claimed to be a historical religion and has attached great importance to the claim that Jesus was a real historical person about whom we have reliable knowledge. This has often been held to distinguish the Christian belief in the incarnation of God in Christ from Egyptian myths of a dying and rising god, from Hindu beliefs in 'avatars' (incarnate deities) coming to earth in ancient pre-history, or from the Pure-land Buddhist belief that the 'heavenly' Amida Buddha became incarnate aeons ago 'in the unremembered past'.[1] By contrast, the life of Jesus has been located in datable and well-documented history, and his birth has been seen as literally the central point of human history. It is axiomatic to orthodoxy that Jesus was fully God, fully human, and a real historical figure. Just how these beliefs were mutually compatible was, of course, a matter of fierce debate in the first five centuries AD. But from Chalcedon until the dawn of the nineteenth century there was a widespread Christian consensus about the truth and intelligibility of such claims. All four Gospels were treated as the archetypes of truthful reporting (Gospel truth!), and both the humanity and the divinity of Jesus seemed to be supported by them. Much in the Gospels clearly testified to Jesus' full humanity, while the infancy narratives, the miracles and the 'I am' sayings in the Fourth Gospel pointed to his divinity. As St Leo declared in 449,

> each nature performs what is proper to itself ... the one is resplendent with miracles, the other succumbs to injuries ... the infancy of the little child is shown by the lowly cradle, the greatness of the Most High is declared by the voices of the angels ... to feel hunger, thirst and weariness is evidently human, but to satisfy thousands of men with five loaves ... to walk on the surface of the sea ... and to rebuke the tempest is without doubt divine.[2]

However, this consensus came to be threatened by the rise of history as an academic discipline. Once the Gospels were subjected to historical scrutiny, it became clear that there was a significant difference between the ethos of the fourth Gospel and that of the other three. It was not easy to reconcile the picture of Jesus in the first three with the picture of Jesus in the fourth. It was noted that even the early Christians had seen this difference, in that, according to Clement of Alexandria, 'last of all seeing that the physical facts had been recorded in the (other) Gospels ... John wrote a spiritual Gospel'.[3] This ancient tradition helped establish a new consensus that if we wanted to know 'the physical facts' about the historical Jesus, we should rely only on the first three Gospels. Historical criticism also showed how common it was in ancient literature for legendary and mythical elements to be mixed in with sober history, and hence that we should approach the miraculous elements in the Gospels with the same critical questioning as we would approach such elements in any other ancient writing. Christian scholars were convinced in the nineteenth century that it was extremely important to use the tools of historical criticism to get back to the earliest, and hence most authentic, reconstruction of the life of Jesus.

In 1901 a century of historical research into both the New Testament and the Patristic period was summed up in the writings of Adolf von Harnack, whose synthesis of 'Liberal Protestant Christianity' became enormously influential in the Modernist movement in Britain. Harnack was unequivocal that authentic Christianity was essentially 'Jesus and his Gospel'. Harnack wrote a seven-volume *History of Dogma* in which he argued that there had been a gradual 'Hellenisation' of Christ's Gospel over the first five centuries AD, in the course of which the simple message of Jesus himself had been transmuted into a vast and complex system of dogma expressed in the categories of Greek philosophy and endorsed by the first four Councils. To rediscover the original Christian message, we need to get back to the teaching of the historical Jesus. Our authorities for this are the first three Gospels understood in their original Jewish context. Harnack spelt out what he thought we can know of the historical Jesus in his most popular work, *What is Christianity?* This identified the 'essence of Christianity' with the teaching of Jesus. This was summed up as a proclamation of the coming of the kingdom of God growing in the hearts of those who respond to the message and who accept Christ's teaching of the fatherhood of God and the brotherhood of all humanity. Harnack believed that the story of the Virgin Birth was not part of the oldest traditions concerning Jesus, and he urged 'more hesitation in our judgement concerning stories of the miraculous'.[4] With regard to the resurrection, he believed that what really mattered was the Easter faith that 'Jesus lives'. Harnack believed that the story of the empty tomb was 'probable' but not something we can be certain about, whereas the appearances of Christ were 'all-important' as leading to the 'indestructible belief that death is vanquished, that there is life eternal'.[5]

On the question of Christology, Harnack believed:

Jesus desired no other belief in his person and no other attachment to it than is contained in the keeping of his commandments ... To lay down any 'doctrine' about his person and his dignity independently of the Gospel was quite outside his sphere of ideas ... He described the Lord of heaven and earth as his father; and as the Creator, and as Him who is alone good. He is certain that everything which he has and everything which he is to accomplish comes from this Father. He prays to Him; he subjects himself to his will; he struggles to find out what it is and to fulfil it. Aim strength, understanding ... must all come from the Father. This is what the Gospels say, and it cannot be turned and twisted. This feeling, praying, working, struggling, and suffering individual is a man who in the face of his God also associates himself with other men.[6]

Harnack was quite sure that, as a matter of history, 'The Gospel as Jesus proclaimed it has to do with the Father only and not with the Son'. However, if we start from the fact of Jesus' human identity, we can also go on to see why he was subsequently seen as a person in whom we see God. For he not only taught the Gospel; 'he was its personal realisation and its strength.' History shows that he is one 'who brings the weary and heavy-laden to God'. Through the way he lived we can see God revealed in the language of a human life; for, according to Harnack, in Jesus 'the divine appeared in as pure a form as it can appear on earth'.[7]

The classic Modernists shared Harnack's belief that we could get back to the historical Jesus, and that the reconstruction of

Jesus' teaching is what Christianity ought to be. A. M. Ramsey notes that much of English theology in the first decades of the twentieth century was 'akin to Harnack, both in critical method and in religious attitude ... [and that] ... many presentations of the life of Jesus were written on these lines, the most influential being T. R. Glover's *The Jesus of History'*.[8] At the Girton Conference of 1921, speaker after speaker affirmed that 'the person of Jesus, the historic Jesus, is real and knowable', and even R. H. Lightfoot affirmed then: 'I do not think we need have any doubt at all, as to His personality or the general nature of His teaching.'[9] Subsequently, B. H. Streeter popularized the four-document hypothesis to explain the background to the Synoptic Gospels. This asserted the priority of Mark and said that in addition to Mark, Matthew and Luke each had their own individual source as well as sharing a common source, referred to as 'Q'. This documentary hypothesis encouraged belief in the historic reliability of the Synoptic Gospels.

Although the Modernists believed we could know a lot about Jesus' teaching in its original Jewish context, they characteristically rejected belief in the infancy narratives, the Virgin Birth, and the ascension of Jesus. They also rationalized the 'nature miracles' and insisted that, though healing miracles could not be excluded, they should be seen as human phenomena rather than as illustrations of any divine power. However, they affirmed a belief in the resurrection of Jesus while denying that this necessarily entailed the emptiness of his tomb. Most controversy associated with the Modernists tended to focus on these points, and it was considered as a major achievement when the Doctrine Report of 1938 accepted the legitimacy of such views within the Church of England.

Yet for many years before 1938 the tide had been running against the Modernists in most areas of New Testament and doctrinal scholarship. In Germany it came to be all but universally accepted that we could not get back behind the teaching of the early Church to see Jesus himself. One reason for abandoning the quest of the historical Jesus was the view of Albert Schweitzer that apocalyptic expectations of the end of the world dominated Jesus' thinking and made him alien to us; another was that the different nineteenth-century lives of Jesus had presented a variety of mutually incompatible pictures of Jesus' personality, and all too often the image presented of Jesus corresponded more closely to the ideals and values of the historian than to what could plausibly be assigned to a first-century Jew. Third, form-criticism encouraged the study of isolated units of tradition which were believed to have initially circulated on their own in the early Church. This led many to think that we cannot get back behind the faith of the early Church to Jesus himself and therefore have no choice but to accept the picture of Christ preached within the Church. This view was initially put forward by Martin Kahler, who said that 'the real Christ was the preached Christ'.[10] We have already seen that such a view was vigorously championed by Karl Barth, whose teaching was generally assumed by most pastors to be a vindication of popular orthodoxy. Similar attitudes also became extremely popular in British theology in the Biblical Theology school. It is paradoxical that a widespread conviction of the impossibility of knowing anything for certain about the historical Jesus was interpreted in practice as a licence to take the historical tradition of the Church concerning him as self-authenticating, as if lack of knowledge of the Jesus of history could be taken to vindicate a traditional understanding of the Christ of Faith.

The person most associated with form-criticism was Rudolf Bultmann, who in his book *Jesus and the Word* declared: 'I do indeed think that we can now know almost nothing concerning the life and teaching of Jesus, since the early Christian sources show no interest in either, are moreover fragmentary and often legendary; and other sources about Jesus do not exist.'[11] Such attitudes dominated New Testament scholarship for decades and the Liberal Protestant and Modernist stress on the historical Jesus came to be thought of as outmoded and irrelevant. According to Geza Vermes, 'Under the colossal influence of Bultmann on German, and subsequently through his students on North American New Testament learning, the clock of real historical research stopped for almost half a century.'[12] The impact on Britain was equally great. R. H. Lightfoot, who had been so confident about what we can know about Jesus in 1921, came to a very different conclusion in 1935 after studying the form-critics:

It seems then that the form of the earthly no less than the heavenly Christ is for the most part hidden from us. For all the inestimable value of the Gospels, they yield us little more than a whisper of his voice, we trace in them but the outskirts of his ways.[13]

Since a generation of biblical scholars up to and including Dennis Nineham studied under Lightfoot, such views became normative in Britain as well as in North America and Germany.

E. P. Sanders believes that for about sixty years the consensus of most New Testament scholarship was fundamentally sceptical. According to him, 'New Testament scholars spent several decades – from about 1910 to 1970 – saying that we know somewhere between very little and virtually nothing about the historical Jesus.'[14] The first sign of a possible change was the publication of Ernst Kasemann's lecture on the problem of the historical Jesus in 1953, followed by the first full-scale post-Bultmannian life of Jesus of Nazareth, by Gunther Bornkamm in 1956.[15] However, both these continue to reflect great uncertainties. A more positive tone was a slow and gradual development. But, as Sanders indicates, 'in recent decades we have grown more confident'. His own position now is: 'There are no substantial doubts about the general course of Jesus' life: when and where he lived, approximately when and where he died, and the sort of thing he did during his public activity.'[16] Sanders's study of *The Historical Figure of Jesus* gives the fullest and most detailed account of the emerging consensus, which is backed up both by the detail of his other works and by the comparably positive conclusions of other scholars such as J. P. Meier, James Dunn, N. T. Wright and Leslie Houlden.[17] This general approach is also supported from a Jewish perspective by Geza Vermes and Martin Goodman. According to Goodman:

> Whatever the problems in reconstructing the life and career of Jesus (and they are immense), it is more plausible than otherwise that the general outline of his career as presented in the Gospel biographies is correct, simply because the hypothesis that these accounts were entirely composed, rather than partially altered, to make a theological point is more implausible than the belief that the outlines of Jesus' career are correctly described.[18]

What is now increasingly recognized is that the Gospel writers, while certainly writing from a perspective of commitment to Jesus, nevertheless were concerned to set down what they genuinely believed to have happened to him. It used to be claimed against treating the Gospels as truly historical that they did not show any interest in the most obvious kinds of biographical detail and description of their subject that today we would regard as axiomatic. Yet, by comparison with other biographies from the Graeco-Roman world, we can see that the Gospels do conform to the expectations of their own age, and compared to writings of a similar kind from the ancient world they may be regarded as reliable sources of information.[19] Sanders points out that, even though Alexander the Great radically altered the political situation of his day while Jesus did not, there are important respects in which we know more about Jesus than we know about Alexander. This is because the sources for Jesus are better, so that we have a much clearer idea of what Jesus thought than of what Alexander thought.[20] A. E. Harvey claims that there are 'certain facts about Jesus which by any normal criterion of historical evidence it would be unreasonable to doubt'.[21] And Graham Stanton argues: 'We do know a good deal about Jesus ... Historians, whether Christian or not, are able to confirm that Jesus did exist and that the evangelists' portraits, for all their differences, are not wholly misleading.'[22]

This does not mean that modern scholarship endorses the traditional picture of Jesus as perceived by the Churches. Historical and literary criticism constantly reminds us of the inevitable limits of our knowledge as we look back over long centuries. But, whereas an earlier generation of scholars tended to say that unless we know something for certain we should not claim to know it at all, the modern view recognizes that uncertainty is present in all historical reconstructions of the past and need be no bar to reasonable confidence in what seems the most probable interpretation of what lies behind the narrative. There is now very substantial agreement among New Testament scholars, whether they be Christian or Jewish or simply historians of ancient thought, that we really know a great deal about Jesus' life and teaching. To read the works of E. P. Sanders and Geza Vermes is to be aware that, when placed in Jesus' own Jewish historical setting, his teaching fits extremely well, and we can now gain a better insight into his religious perspective and understanding. We may also come to appreciate what Vermes calls 'the magnetic appeal of the teaching and example of Jesus'.[23] The tone of modern historical scholarship is thus very much more confident than that of earlier generations, and it is clear that historical criticism can genuinely help us to a fuller knowledge of the actual life, work and teaching of the founder of Christianity.

While saying that we now have fuller knowledge of the 'founder of Christianity' is in one sense true, however, it is also misleading. Stanton robustly points out that 'Jesus certainly did not intend to found a new religion',[24] and Vermes adds that he would have been utterly mystified by most of the articles of the Nicene Creed, which 'appear to have little to do with the religion preached and practised by him'.[25] The problem, basically, is that the contemporary study of Jesus raises in an even more acute form all the problems that the old quest of the historical Jesus had brought up – and the most central of these problems is the connection between the Jesus of History and the Christ of Faith. I have called this book *The Contemporary Challenge of Modernist Theology*. In connection with New Testament scholarship this title seems apt because, although the neutral detached scholarship of our own day has no identification with any such Church party, the issues that its work raises are very similar to those that the Modernists urged the Churches to address seventy years ago. It would be a bewildering paradox if the institution that came into existence ostensibly to continue Jesus' work should ignore what historical research now shows us to have been his teaching.

Harnack and Vermes are in complete agreement that, with regard to the historical Jesus, 'research has to be restricted to Mark, Matthew and Luke, and to exclude John because, despite the occasional historical detail it contains, John is so evolved theologically as to be wholly unsuitable for historical investigation'.[26] This carries the challenge to the Churches that any understanding of Jesus' divinity which is based on the 'I am' sayings of John lacks any historical foundation. As Adrian Thatcher points out, 'There is scarcely a single competent New Testament scholar who is prepared to defend the view that the four instances of the absolute use of "I am" in John . . . can be historically attributed to Jesus.'[27] Likewise, there is full agreement with the Modernist claim that the historical Jesus had no thought of himself as being divine. Even a relatively conservative scholar such as James Dunn admits that there is 'no real evidence in the earliest Jesus tradition of what could fairly be called a consciousness of divinity'.[28] We shall see later that, if this is true, it ought to have a profound impact on how one understands the claims relating to divine incarnation in Jesus.

The Modernists were most criticized in their own day for their rejection of the story of the Virgin Birth and of the stress on miracles in the Gospels. Once again, this is the standard view of contemporary scholarship. It is significant that Kasemann, Ernst Fuchs and James Robinson, who pioneered the new quest of the historical Jesus, simply omit the infancy narratives.[29] Gunther Bornkamm claims that they are 'too much overgrown by legends ... and messianic conceptions to be used for historical assertions'[30] and Leslie Houlden argues that they are 'late ... inconsistent with each other ... and almost wholly dependent on prophetic texts'.[31] Almost all the books that seek to justify belief in the essential historicity of Jesus' life do not refer to them. This is not really surprising. The problems with the infancy narratives are not simply the supernatural elements such as a birth from a virgin, or the presence of angels in the narrative, or the location of a star being usable in identifying a house on earth, but also that even the most prosaic elements challenge credulity. What, for instance, was a sane ruler like Augustus doing in issuing a decree that all descendants of King David should go to Bethlehem to be taxed? King David had died 960 years earlier, and his dynasty had been replaced several times. To issue such a decree would be almost akin to Margaret Thatcher saying that, in order to ensure collection of poll tax, everyone who could prove their descent from the Old Saxon royal family should go to Winchester to pay it! There is almost total agreement among scholars that the infancy narratives are simply Jewish Midrash woven out of Old Testament prophecies. As conservative a scholar as G. B. Caird argues that 'we do Luke a grave injustice if we suppose that when he wrote in an elevated and imaginative style, he was naive enough to take his own poetry with pedantic literalness'.[32]

Miracle stories pose rather different issues. Most people in the ancient world believed in miracle and magic, and consequently miracle stories were regularly associated with holy men and religious teachers in both the Jewish and the Gentile world. It is not surprising, therefore, that such stories are told about Jesus. There is no need for total scepticism in relation to surprising healings, in that there is plenty of evidence for the psychosomatic character of much spontaneous remission of illness. On the other hand, historians do not take seriously the accounts of nature miracles like walking on the water or multiplying loaves and fishes, since these conflict too seriously with what we know of the uniformity of nature. What is common both to the Modernists of the early years of the century and to contemporary New Testament scholarship is that if Jesus did bring about some surprising cures both would see this as attributable to the force of his human personality rather than to any divine attributes. Geza Vermes points out that historically the Synoptic Gospels' picture of Jesus as 'a popular teacher, healer and exorcist . . . fits perfectly into the first-century Galilee known directly from Josephus, and indirectly from rabbinic literature. He represents the charismatic Judaism of wonder-working holy men such as the first century BC Honi and Jesus' younger contemporary, Hanina ben Dosa', all of whom were believed able to 'feed the hungry and cure disease physical and mental'.[33]

The resurrection of Jesus is an issue which requires a chapter in its own right, in relation both to the views of the classic Modernists and to the contemporary debate. But in both cases the resurrection is seen as crucial to our understanding of the historical Jesus. Barth denied this, arguing that the resurrection 'cannot be thought of as history' because as an 'autonomous new act of God' it contains 'no component of human action'.[34] The problem with Barth's position is that, in making the resurrection an event outside history, he empties it of all intelligibility. If the resurrection of Jesus 'happened', which Barth wishes to affirm, then he must be willing to affirm that it happened in history, or words cease to have meaning. Similarly, Bultmann's suggestion that the resurrection be understood 'simply as an attempt to convey the meaning of the cross'[35] should be rejected because it simply does not make any sense of the subsequent Christian proclamation as exemplified in 1 Corinthians 15. The cross without what Christians believe to have been its sequel would have been a very different thing. The resurrection of Jesus is a complex and controversial theme but it is centrally a historical issue. As Sanders says, 'that Jesus' followers (and later Paul) had resurrection experiences is in my judgement a fact'. However, he goes on to say 'what the reality was that gave rise to the experiences I don't know'. But it is clear that he sees it as important, because he believes it created the Christian movement.[36]

The historical story of Jesus is not the end-point for Christian theology. But both for the Modernists of the early years of this century and for some of the most important strands of contemporary Christian theology the historical Jesus is the essential starting-point. Alistair McGrath points out that, according to Joachim Jeremias, the basis of Christian faith lies in what Jesus actually said and did in so far as this can be established by theological scholarship.[37] This theme has become increasingly dominant in contemporary New Testament studies. For example, the SCM list of new books from February to July 1998 contained no fewer than seven which related to the historical Jesus. Moreover, the Jesus now emerging is a vastly more credible and exciting figure than the Jesus of the former liberals. Much as I admire Harnack, it really sounds bathetically trite to sum up Jesus' teaching with a platitude such as the fatherhood of God and the brotherhood of man. And a major problem of some of the Modernist accounts of the 1920s, such as that of F. J. Foakes-Jackson and Kirsopp Lake, is that they succeeded in making Jesus 'merely dull'[38] or seemed to present him as simply 'a teacher of virtue and morals for a better bourgeois life'.[39]

However, such an accusation cannot be made against some of the dynamic pictures of Jesus made in recent decades. Of these by far the most influential has been the brilliant presentation made by Hans Kung in his greatest book, *On Being a Christian*. According to Kung, the distinctive message of Christianity is not the Christ of dogma or the Christ of piety but the real Christ, the historical person, Jesus the Jew, 'who was wholly and entirely concerned with God'.[40] Kung has no doubt at all that the centre of Christianity is what the historical Jesus taught and proclaimed about God's cause. And he describes this in terms which show why Jesus has had such an impact on human history and why his message still challenges us to new life. Kung also makes clear why Jesus came to be seen as the 'human face of God' and why if we start 'from below' with the historical Jesus we will also come to understand why 'this true man, Jesus of Nazareth is for faith the real revelation of the one true God'.[41] To explore this further, let us move on from the Jesus of History and see how this understanding of Jesus can also help to make sense of the Christian claims concerning his divinity.

7

Modern ways of understanding the divinity of Christ

The contemporary confidence of New Testament scholarship in our knowledge of the historical Jesus in the setting of the religious life and thought of his own time poses a significant challenge to traditional Christianity. Indeed, Geza Vermes sees it as the greatest challenge of all, coming as it does from Jesus himself![1] It is in essence the same challenge as was made by Harnack in 1901 or by the early Modernists at their conference on 'Christ and the Creeds' in 1921. But it is now much more powerful, both because it can no longer be represented as the maverick opinions of a few Modern Churchmen, and because the picture of Jesus revealed by contemporary scholarship is much more obviously the picture of a first-century Jew than the somewhat less authentic portraits painted by earlier liberals. That we know a great deal about the historical Jesus is now the mainstream view of contemporary scholarship. As early as 1974 Hans Kung could talk of the emerging of a far-reaching agreement on exegetical questions which embraced not only 'progressive German scholars' but also 'the more conservative Anglo-Saxon and French'.[2] The reason why this emerging consensus is a threat to traditional Christianity is that its understanding of the personhood of the Jesus of History differs significantly from the way that has been understood within the mainstream of the Christian tradition.

To clarify this, let me spell out the interpretation of the doctrine of Christ that has been widely accepted as normative in the Christian Church since at least the Second Council of Constantinople of AD 553. This Council made explicit what may, or may not, have been the view of Chalcedon in 451, that the 'personhood' of Jesus Christ was exclusively of divine origin. Jesus was, in the fullest possible sense, 'True God, the Lord of Glory and one of the Holy Trinity'.[3] The Council claimed that at the same time Jesus Christ was fully human in that he possessed all the attributes of our humanity. But it said that in the case of Jesus Christ, his human nature was 'owned' not by a human-subject *hypostasis* but by the incarnate Logos of God. This understanding of the incarnation assumes that it is intelligible to suppose that there can be a substantial *hypostatic* union of the divine and human natures in the one person of Christ, and that there can be a communion of the properties of each *communicatio idiomatum*, such that, though the human and divine natures remain separate, the attributes of the one may be predicated in the other by virtue of their union in the one person of the Saviour.[4] E. L. Mascall, a stalwart defender of such notions, claims that the possibility of distinguishing between the human nature of Christ and its metaphysical divine subject is a *sine qua non* for the doctrine of the atonement. He reminds us of the teaching of St Gregory Nazianzus that 'we needed an incarnate God, a God put to death that we might live'.[5] Yet since the personhood of God logically cannot suffer or die, it was necessary for the Godhead also to assume a nature in which this could happen. So, according to Mascall, 'the assumption of a real and complete human nature by the person of God the Son ... provided the impassible God with a nature in which he could really suffer'.[6]

The concept of the divine Son having two mutually communicating natures also served another useful function, in that it enabled Christ, while living under the restriction of a human life in one nature, to continue to have access to divine power and knowledge in his other nature. Hence, St Thomas Aquinas could claim that, although Jesus in his human nature gained empirical knowledge through the senses just as we do, nevertheless at the same time he also had access through his divine nature to the unlimited knowledge of God: 'With perfect insight he beheld all God's works, past, present and future ... he sees in God everything God does and in this sense can be called omniscient.'[7] Moreover, he lived all his life in the full knowledge of his part in the divine plan of redemption: 'He the Lord and maker of history chose his time [to be born], his birthplace and his mother ... His manner of life was shaped to the purpose of his incarnation, because as he himself proclaimed, "for this I was born and for this I came into the world, that I should bear testimony to the truth"'.[8]

This picture of the incarnation certainly presents us with

'Christ, the power of God and the wisdom of God',[9] but in no sense does it present us with one who was 'made like his brethren in every respect'.[10] It is true that all orthodox writers pay lip-service to Christ's humanity and describe him as 'consubstantial with us' in his human nature. But all meaning seems evacuated from these claims when Christ is denied any human individuality or subjectivity. To know oneself as pre-existently and eternally divine and as possessing all knowledge and all power is simply incompatible with sharing in the experience of the limitations of a human life. As such, the tradition as expounded at the Second Council of Constantinople and developed in Christian thought over the next thousand years represents a betrayal of the earlier concern to safeguard the reality of Christ's true humanity. Consequently it fails to articulate a coherent theory of the incarnation; for in what sense could a supposedly pre-existent divine Christ really be said to have become 'fully human' if he continued to have access to divine power and knowledge? On the other hand, if he had *no* access to divine power or knowledge, in what sense could he still be divine?

What can be established for certain is that the historical Jesus was definitely not omniscient. His knowledge was restricted to that available to his generation. In the history of thought this has usually been illustrated by highlighting trivial errors such as the fact that Jesus attributed to King David a Psalm which Old Testament scholarship shows must be ascribed to a much later period,[11] or that Jesus thought that salt could lose its savour, which of course it cannot.[12] Much more importantly, however, he took for granted that epilepsy was caused by demonic possession and shared the apocalyptic expectation of his contemporaries that the end of all things would come within the lifetime of those who heard him speak.[13]

In 1921 Hastings Rashdall laid down five essential preliminaries for any discussion of 'Christ as Logos and as Son of God', in the light of what seemed to be the clear findings of New Testament scholarship. These were (1) Jesus did not formally claim divinity for himself; (2) Jesus was in the fullest sense a man; (3) it is untrue that the human soul of Jesus pre-existed; (4) the Virgin Birth is not necessarily implied in the incarnation; (5) nor is the omniscience of Jesus on earth. Although these statements were generally thought to be deeply controversial at the time and might still occasion press comment if made publicly by a bishop, they are all commonplaces of contemporary scholarship and are presuppositions accepted by almost all contemporary theologians.

For most scholars, accepting these facts requires a reinterpretation of what is meant by the incarnation. However, some believe it is possible to continue to affirm the traditional understanding of Jesus as a literally divine person while accepting the findings of modern biblical scholarship. They do this by adopting the theory of *kenosis* or 'emptying'. This is based on 1 Philippians 2: 6–8, which says of Jesus that: 'though he was in the form of God he did not count equality with God a thing to be grasped but *emptied himself*, taking the form of a servant'. According to adherents of the theory of *kenosis,* the eternal and pre-existent divine Christ emptied himself of all his divine power, knowledge and self-awareness of divinity in the process of becoming incarnate. On this basis it is claimed that one can accept everything that modern scholarship has told us of the real humanity of the historical Jesus and yet continue to claim that the subject of Christ's personhood was exclusively divine.

In British theology the doctrine of *kenosis* was pioneered by Charles Gore at the end of the nineteenth century and was much discussed in the early years of the century. It remains extremely popular among many contemporary theologians. They accept the consensus of New Testament scholarship that the Synoptic Gospels give us a better insight into the Jesus of History than St John's Gospel does, and hence they reject the claims to divinity implicit in the 'I am' sayings of that Gospel. They see the miracle stories as part of the human history of Jesus rather than as pointers to any divine status. And they stress how much of Jesus' thought and teaching was conditioned by the thought-forms and knowledge of his day, so that both ignorance and error may be attributed to him. But, in spite of all this, they acclaim him as literally God incarnate. John Austin Baker, for example, is wholly committed to the incarnation, and yet he believes that the Gospel records allow us to claim neither sinlessness nor infallibility for the historical Jesus. Indeed, he explicitly criticizes Jesus' moral stance and states that Jesus was mistaken about the programme that God planned to follow. Baker argues that any true doctrine of the incarnation would be destroyed if we imagine for a moment

that Jesus was ever conscious of being God: 'It is simply not possible to share the common lot of humanity and be aware of oneself
as one who has existed from everlasting.'[14] Likewise, Brian
Hebblethwaite insists that Jesus shared all the limitations of
human psychology and knowledge, and yet supposes that as God
he came among us incognito to win our response:[15]

> God himself, without ceasing to be God, has come among us,
> not just in but as a man, at a particular time and place. The
> human life lived and the death died have been held quite literal-
> ly to be the human life and death of God himself in one of the
> modes of his eternal being.[16]

The difficulty with this position is that is self-contradictory.
One cannot simultaneously affirm that Jesus gave up all his divine
attributes and also that he did this 'without ceasing to be God'. As
Hastings Rashdall pointed out long ago, kenoticists are committed to the view that 'up to the moment of the Incarnation' the pre-
existent Christ knew

> everything – all history, all modern science, all the undiscovered
> science there is yet to know ... but from the moment of the
> Incarnation He knew this no more for thirty-three years. Now it
> is surely a difficult doctrine to maintain that such a colossal loss
> of memory, such a complete break of consciousness in the Son
> was consistent with what we call personal identity.[17]

It seems to me that Rashdall's case is unanswerable, and to illustrate this we might recall that it was precisely for this reason that
Christianity rejected the ancient Pythagorean belief in reincarnation. As St Irenaeus put it, 'We may subvert their doctrine as to
transmigration from body to body by this fact, that souls remember nothing whatsoever of the events which took place in their
previous state.'[18] Precisely the same considerations apply when
considering the logic of belief in the incarnation of a pre-existent
divine being on earth as when considering the logic of belief in the
reincarnation of a former human being on earth. In both cases,
without any memory of the supposed former life the concept of
such a life becomes wholly meaningless.

The problem with the kenotic theory is not just the question of
continuity of identity through such a monumental change; there is

also the question of why anyone should suppose that Jesus should be regarded as divine in this absolute sense after all the traditional 'pointers' to his divinity have been repudiated. After all, modern kenotic scholars do not believe that Jesus was heralded by prophets or vindicated by miracles; nor do they attribute to him sinlessness, infallibility or divine consciousness. So how do we know that this man rather than any other is God living incognito in our midst? The only answer given is faith in Jesus' resurrection. But can this be enough to ensure his identification with God? Is rising from the dead so very different in status from the ascension into heaven attributed in Jewish tradition to Enoch, Elijah or Moses? Moreover, consider G. B. Caird's illuminating exercise in imagination:

> Let us suppose that tomorrow you were confronted with irrefutable evidence that an acquaintance whom you had good reason to believe dead had been seen alive by a reliable witness. You would certainly feel compelled to revise your ideas about God. I doubt that you would conclude that your acquaintance was divine, or that a stamp of authenticity had been placed on all that he ever said and did.[19]

If one already had an exalted concept of the person of Christ, then belief in his resurrection might well serve as the coping-stone holding together the edifice of personal faith in him. But, taken on its own, it simply cannot carry the weight placed upon it by some contemporary Christian scholars. I conclude that once Jesus' life is viewed in its historical setting there cease to be any valid grounds for claiming that a wholly divine 'person' was the real subject of Jesus' life although even Jesus himself was unaware of this! An 'incognito' as complete as this simply empties the traditional doctrine of all meaning. The *language* of traditional doctrine is preserved in all kenotic Christologies, but the meaning has been 'emptied out' of the doctrine along with the removal of all the divine attributes.

Although the Modernists of the 1920s, as well as many contemporary theologians, reject both the traditional understanding of the incarnation and the kenoticists' reinterpretation of it, they still see themselves as believers in the incarnation. Their claim is that to deny the classic account of the incarnation is not to deny the incarnation itself. We saw in the first chapter that the Modernists were totally committed to the view that 'God was in Christ.' They had no doubt that the Christian Gospel teaches that Jesus is proclaimed in some sense as both God and man. The real question for them is what such an affirmation meant in practice. They suggested that it should be understood as making a claim that Jesus has the value of God for us in that Jesus leads us to know God, and that through Jesus' consciousness of God 'the divine appeared in as pure a form as it can appear on earth', so that 'for those who followed him Jesus was the strength of the Gospel'.[20]

The first important contribution made by the Modernists was to draw attention to what the Logos doctrine originally meant. The title 'Jesus, Word of God Incarnate' has certainly come to be interpreted in an absolute sense as having reference to Jesus alone, but that was not its original meaning. 'Word' is the translation of the Greek *Logos,* which in Stoic philosophy means that spark of the divine present in every human soul. In the Old Testament the 'Word of the Lord' is said to have come to each of the prophets and to have been the source of their insights. Hence, whether the author of the Fourth Gospel was thinking in Hellenistic or in Hebrew terms, the expression 'the Logos' would have had a wide significance for him. It would at least have meant that the divine 'Word' which found expression in the life of Christ was that same 'Word of God' which had spoken through the prophets. It might also have had a much deeper connotation. The most natural reading of John 1: 9 proclaims that the Logos which became incarnate in Christ was 'the true light which enlightens every man who comes into the world'. On this translation, the prologue to the Fourth Gospel explicitly affirms the Stoic doctrine of the universal Logos. And even on the alternative translation, which says that 'the true light which enlightens every man was even then coming into the world', there are implicit echoes of the Stoic philosophy.[21]

Within the early Church, Christian theologians who lived and worked in the context of Greek thought were always aware that talk of Christ as the Logos of God did not imply that the Logos was *only* present in the earthly Jesus. St Athanasius, for example, insisted that the incarnation of the divine Logos in Christ did not mean that it was 'hedged in by Jesus' body, nor did his presence in the body prevent his being present elsewhere as well'.[22] We may take Athanasius as representative of all the Greek Fathers in stressing that the real presence of God in Christ in no way implied any diminution of God's continuing activity throughout the universe. Hence, there is no question of numerical identity between God and Jesus implied in the doctrine of the incarnation. Acceptance of the ongoing activity of the divine Logos carries the consequence that throughout Jesus' ministry 'the light that enlightens every man'[23] was as active as ever in the hearts and minds of men and women throughout the world. The full implications of this were spelt out by Archbishop William Temple in 1939, when he applied the Logos doctrine to world religion and insisted that 'By the Word of God – that is to say by Jesus Christ – Isaiah, and Plato, and Zoroaster, and Buddha, and Confucius conceived and uttered such truths as they declared. There is only one divine light; and every man in his measure is enlightened by it.'[24] Yet to accept that in some sense the Logos is at least potentially present in every human being profoundly affects what might be meant by the claim that the Logos became incarnate in Christ.

In addition to the implications of the Logos doctrine we might also observe that it is a logical deduction from belief in God's omniscience that a truly all-knowing God will know 'my every inward thought and feeling', as the Requiem Mass affirms. If this is true, then one can legitimately ask whether the in-dwelling of the Logos in Jesus was different in kind or merely in degree from his in-dwelling in other people. Consider the sense of God's reality as experienced by the author of Psalm 139:

> Lord, you have examined me and you know me
> You know everything that I do . . .
> You understand all my thoughts . . .
> You know all my actions.
> Even before I speak you already know what I shall say. . .
> Your knowledge of me is too deep
> It is beyond my understanding.

It is hard to see how any sense of the presence of God could be more vivid than this, even to the historical Jesus. At most, we might speculate that this overwhelming sense of the reality of God which ideally should exist at all times between the individual and the creator did in fact always exist in Jesus. But to embrace this conclusion is to admit a difference of degree rather than of kind in the nature of Jesus' knowledge of God. And to argue for a difference of degree rather than kind is precisely the view championed by the Modernists in what is probably their greatest contribution to twentieth-century discussion of Christology.

The idea of a degree Christology starts from the conviction that in all human beings there is a spark of the divine light even if in most it is obscured and darkened by self-centredness and sin. Nevertheless, in the presence of a holy or saintly person one can sometimes feel aware of the presence of God at work in that person's life. The more holy the person, is the more likely it is that one will be conscious of God's grace at work within them. Rudolf Otto has shown the very important part played in human religious experiencing by the sense of the holy or numinous through which people encounter the divine. He draws attention to the fact that in the Gospel narrative the numinous object is Jesus Christ. Thus, when Simon Peter first encountered Jesus his immediate response was 'depart from me for I am a sinful man O Lord', and the centurion at Capernaum instinctively felt unworthy that Christ should enter under his roof.[25] In Mark 10: 32 we read: 'and Jesus went before them: and they were amazed; and as they followed they were afraid'. Otto comments: 'This passage renders with supreme simplicity and force the immediate impression of the numinous that issued from the man Jesus.' He suggests that in this response to Jesus we see 'the real roots of all later developments of Christology'.[26]

According to Hastings Rashdall, 'in the conditions of the highest human life, we have access as nowhere else to the inmost nature of the divine'. But, he insists, 'it is impossible to maintain that God is fully incarnate in Christ and not incarnate at all in anyone else'.[27] Rather, Rashdall presents the idea of the in-dwelling power of God at work in all human lives, but in varying degrees: 'men do not reveal God equally ... the higher and more developed moral consciousness reveals him more than the lower, and above all the actually better man reveals God more than the worse man'. In Jesus we 'discover the highest revelation of the divine nature'.[28]

In the history of thought the claims of a degree Christology came to be rejected because Charles Gore claimed that it implied that the difference between God and human beings was only a matter of degree. His justification for saying this was that two leading Modernists, Henry Major and J. F. Bethune Baker, had spoken loosely in this way.[29] However, properly understood a degree Christology in no way blurs the difference between God and humankind. Rashdall is clear that that which is a matter of degree is the human knowledge of God, and the extent to which that consciousness or awareness of the divine leads to an indwelling of God's spirit. Understood in this sense, the theory make as good sense today as when it was first put forward. John Hick argues that a degree Christology greatly helps an understanding of the person of Christ:

> If the entirety of the divine nature can co-exist with human nature in one person, then less than the entirety of the divine nature can presumably even more easily co-exist with human nature. It becomes an almost inevitable conclusion that to the degree that other men are Christ-like, to that extent God is incarnate in them also. Incarnation then becomes a matter of degree: God is incarnate in all men in so far as they are Spirit-filled or Christ-like.[30]

The hypothesis of a degree Christology starts from two widely agreed facts about the historical Jesus and his impact: namely, that Jesus had no sense of being divine, and that people did nevertheless become aware of God through him. The hypothesis also accepts as a fact of religious experiencing that people can become aware of God through his presence in the lives of others. Rashdall suggested that in Jesus the divine presence we partially sense in other holy people was present to the nth degree. Understood this way, it can truly be believed that God was in Christ and yet that Christ was fully human. This understanding of the incarnation is of particular importance in the inter-faith context of today. It places Jesus within the continuum of human religious experiencing, rather than making him totally distinct and alien from the rest of humanity. In this sense the divinity of Christ might become potentially acceptable to Jews, Muslims and Hindus; for in each of these religions there are those who believe that prophets or gurus or other sanctified people can reveal something of God to other human beings. Another advantage of a degree Christology is that it makes intelligible a claim often made for incarnational theology: namely, that in Jesus the personality of God was expressed in the language of a human life. This would only seem possible if the presence of God in Christ was akin to that which we are all capable in principle of experiencing. This is precisely what a degree Christology affirms, and hence this theory has a real contribution to make to our understanding of human experience.

It remains the case that a degree Christology denies that Jesus was consubstantial with God, and to some this implies a denial of an essential Christian truth. At this point one very helpful analogy has been offered by Frances Young. She points out that in the Middle Ages it was assumed that the only way Christ could be really present in the Eucharist was if the substance of the bread and wine actually changed into the substance of the body and blood of Christ, leaving only the outward appearance or 'accidents' of continuing bread and wine remaining.[31] However, nowadays only the most conservative of Roman Catholics would continue to insist that belief in a 'Real Presence' of Christ in the Eucharist depended on accepting this doctrine of 'transubstantiation'. Most are quite happy to believe that in a mysterious, sacramental or metaphorical, but very real, sense we do take Christ into our lives through the sacred elements. The point of this analogy is the claim that, just as we can believe in a real presence of Christ in the Eucharist without affirming the doctrine of *transubstantiation*, so we can believe in the real presence of God in Christ without affirming a doctrine of *consubstantiation*. Both doctrines in their classic form depend on Greek metaphysics about the meaning of substance, and neither squares readily with any contemporary understanding of what substance means. Another parallel between the two doctrines is the fact that in several forms of the Eucharistic prayer the priest asks that 'these gifts of bread and wine may be *to us* the body and blood of Christ'. For this is extremely analogous to the claim of liberal theologians that Christ is *to us* the revelation of God, even though they deny a literal concept of divine incarnation.

Opponents of liberalism ask how God can really be in Christ if the personal consubstantiality of Christ and God is denied. Several answers have been given. Schleiermacher, the father of modern theology, argued that Jesus' awareness of God was so strong that it determined his every thought and action. It follows from this that the personality of God found expression in Jesus' life. We assess personality and form our judgements about people by observing their behaviour. Since what Jesus said and did was always determined by what he thought God wanted him to say and do, his life reveals not only his own human personality but also the personality of God. For Schleiermacher, 'to ascribe to Christ an absolutely powerful God-consciousness, and to attribute to Him an existence of God in Him are exactly the same thing'.[32] On this basis we can legitimately claim, with St Irenaeus, that in Christ we see 'the glory of God in a living man, and the life of that man is the vision of God'.[33]

For D. M. Baillie, the presence of God is better explained not by Jesus' awareness of God, but by God's grace reaching down to him. Baillie points out that all the greatest saints have attributed their good deeds not to themselves, but to God's grace at work in their lives. This does not mean that their actions were not their own. As Baillie says, 'Never is human action more truly and fully personal ... than in those moments of which he can say as a Christian that whatever good was in them was not his but God's.' Baillie believes that this 'paradox of faith' reached its zenith in the life of Christ, who 'surpassed all others in refusing to claim anything for Himself and ascribing all the goodness to God'. As a result of the total attribution of everything to the divine grace at work in him, we can legitimately say that 'the life of Jesus ... being the perfection of humanity, is also ... in a deeper and prior sense the very life of God'.[34]

For Adolf von Harnack, belief in the divinity of Christ is based on a pragmatic assessment of his impact:

> History shows that he is the one who brings the weary and heavy laden to God; and again that he it was raised mankind to the new level ... No one who accepts the Gospel and tries to understand him who gave it to us can fail to affirm that here the divine appeared in as pure a form as it can appear on earth, or to feel that for those who followed him Jesus was himself the strength of the Gospel.[35]

A similar pragmatism influenced the English Modernists, who believed that Jesus can rightly be called divine because it is through him that we gain our fullest insight into God.[36]

Hans Kung is 'against all attempts to deify Jesus', who was 'wholly and utterly man'. Nevertheless, he believes that there is a sense in which it is correct to talk of Jesus as 'truly God', because God was 'present, at work speaking, acting and definitely revealing himself in this Jesus who came among men as God's advocate

and deputy, representative and delegate, and was confirmed by
God as the Crucified raised to life'. Kung believes that the function of the traditional statements of the Church

> about divine sonship, pre-existence, creation mediatorship and
> incarnation – often clothed in the mythological and semi-
> mythological forms of the time – are meant ... to do no more
> and no less than to substantiate the uniqueness, underivability
> and unsurpassability of the call, offer and claim, made in and
> known with Jesus, ultimately not of human but of divine origin
> and therefore absolutely reliable.

In other words, talk of Jesus' divinity is for Kung a way of talking
about 'the permanently reliable absolute standard' of Jesus'
teaching through which God has revealed himself. Kung believed
that his position 'deducted nothing' from 'the truth taught by the
ancient Christological Councils' but simply expressed that truth
in ways which make sense to 'the mental climate of our own
time'.[37]

John Hick argues that talk of divine incarnation in Jesus should
be understood as metaphorically true. Just as 'Winston Churchill
incarnated the British will to resist Hitler', so 'Jesus incarnated
God's love and revealed God's purpose and will'. Jesus was able
to do this because he was exceptionally open and responsive to
the divine presence. The truth of the metaphor 'depends on it
being literally true that Jesus lived in obedient response to the
divine presence, and that he lived a life of unselfish love'.[38]

In looking at all these various attempts to continue to talk of the
divinity of Christ, two issues come to mind. First it must be
acknowledged that these reinterpretations say *less* than the tradition has always wished to affirm about his deity. But this seems
inescapable. The historical evidence about the humanity of Jesus,
which the Church has always recognized to be of crucial importance, as well as our contemporary understanding of what it means
to be a person, both preclude the notion that there could be such a
thing as an impersonal human nature, particularly of one whom
historical research has made so alive and real to us. However, there
is also another problem with these reinterpretations, and that is
that they all say *more* than the historical record warrants. If we take
seriously the findings of the new quest of the historical Jesus we
have no adequate grounds to talk of an 'absolutely powerful God-

consciousness', or to claim that he 'surpassed all others' in his openness to divine grace. We simply cannot know that in Christ 'the divine appeared in as pure a form as it can appear on earth' or that his teaching was of a 'permanently reliable absolute standard'.

It is clear that the figure of the historical Jesus that emerges from the researches of contemporary scholarship is an impressive personality. Sanders confirms that Jesus 'regarded himself as having full authority to speak and act on behalf of God . . . and of being empowered to call people to follow him'.[39] Vermes speaks of the 'magnetic appeal of the teaching and example of Jesus'.[40] Other scholars who are themselves committed Christians will say more than this. But, as Hick has pointed out, we simply do not have the evidence to justify the claims to unique or absolute authority that have been made on Jesus' behalf.[41]

In this situation the Modernist's concept of a 'degree Christology' ought to come into its own. As a matter of history the classic Modernists of the Girton Conference of 1921 were as keen as any others to absolutize Jesus and to talk of his unique-ness (though this was not true of those who attended the fiftieth-anniversary conference in 1967).[42] However, to take seriously a degree Christology means that absolute claims become redun-dant. It is reasonable to claim that the life and teaching of Jesus of Nazareth have had an enormous impact on the religious experi-ence of the human race. It is perfectly legitimate for a Christian believer to feel that we know much more about God's character and purpose because of Jesus' life and teaching, and indeed we also know that this influence has gone much wider than the limits of the Christian Church. As the fact of the millennium reminds us, Jesus has changed history. It would therefore be entirely justifi-able to claim that, to a greater degree than anyone else in human history (so far!), Jesus has revealed God to us. But if the presence of God in human beings is a matter of degree rather than kind, one has no right to talk of uniqueness or absoluteness, and can therefore see Jesus within the continuum of religious thought and experience as one who has revealed God to us through the language of his human life.

8

The Modernist understanding of the resurrection of Jesus Christ

The Modernists had a fairly clear cut 'party line' about the resurrection of Jesus. Hastings Rashdall wrote on 'Resurrection and Immortality' in 1898, the foundation year of what became the Modern Churchpeople's Union. He rejected the idea of physical resurrection in favour of a spiritual one on the grounds that St Paul's testimony concerning the resurrection appearances was forty years earlier than the empty-tomb narratives and that St Paul's account of the 'Resurrection vision is of a kind that can hardly appeal to those who are not already at least predisposed to the belief in human immortality.'[1] Kirsopp Lake, in his survey of *The Historical Evidence for the Resurrection of Jesus* in 1907, came to very negative conclusions about the empty-tomb narratives but was convinced that the New Testament evidence points to the apprehension of a 'spiritual being' rather than of something 'physical and material';[2] though, as Archbishop Carnley points out, Lake found it very hard to say how it was that a spiritual being could be apprehended by the disciples.[3] B. H. Streeter wrestled with the same problem in his contribution to a controversial book of essays called *Foundations* in 1912. Streeter also placed all his emphasis on the resurrection appearances of Jesus rather than on the story of the empty tomb. However, Streeter was less vague on how Christ might have been 'seen'. He believed that the appearances of Jesus were visions 'directly caused by the Lord himself veritably alive and personally in communion with them'. On this view, Jesus' conquest of death should be understood in terms of the immortality of his soul or, in Streeter's own phrase, his 'personal immortality'. Christ's resurrection would then consist in the fact that he was able

to convince the disciples of his victory over death by some

adequate manifestation; possibly by showing Himself to them in some form such as might be covered by St Paul's phrase 'a spiritual body' or possibly through some psychological channel similar to that which explains the mysterious means of communication between persons commonly known as telepathy.[4]

Henry Major excited considerable controversy for his outright denial of the physical resurrection of Jesus, and was publicly accused of heresy for so doing. His justification of his position, set forth in his book *A Resurrection of Relics,* was recognized as a permissible viewpoint within the Church of England by a commission of four theology professors established by the bishop of Oxford,[5] but that things reached such a pitch shows how concerned people were by his position. John Lithgow, in his MA thesis on the early Modernists, suggests that this challenge to Major was one reason why the Modernists closed ranks on this issue. Lithgow documents fully that all the leading Modernists argued for an understanding of the resurrection based on the appearances of Jesus and not contingent on any belief in the empty tomb.[6] It was extremely important to the Modernists that the Doctrine Commission of the Church of England, set up in 1922 by the archbishops of Canterbury and York at least in part because of controversy on this issue, ultimately recognized the legitimacy of their position. According to the *Doctrine Report* of 1938 it was recognized that, while belief that Jesus had risen from the dead was an essential part of the Christian message, this truth was compatible with 'a variety of critical views' on what had actually happened. The majority were content to affirm the 'traditional explanation that the tomb was empty', but they recognized that 'others of us would maintain ... that the general freedom long claimed and used in the interpretation of the clause "the resurrection of the flesh" *carnis resurrectionem* cannot leave the interpretation of the other clause, "the third day he rose again from the dead," unaffected'. They concluded that, in view of the 'complications of the discussion ... it was not surprising that opinions should differ ... on how much in the record is ... derived from ... fact ... and how much is due ... to interpretation'. They felt that, however good the historical record were, 'there would still be room for difference of judgement on how much was seen with the bodily eye and how much with spiritual vision'.[7]

The Commission recognized that a powerful factor in leading some of their members to question the traditional belief was that 'both in the Apostles' Creed and the Pauline Epistles the resurrection of the dead and the Resurrection of Christ were made correlative the one to the other, and that the beliefs are linked not only by their historical origin but also by their essential nature'. This was a recognition of an argument which had been absolutely central to the Modernists' concern for the need to revise the Church's understanding of Jesus' resurrection: namely, that the coherence of Christian doctrine required that was what believed to have happened to Jesus must be related to what we can reasonably expect to happen to ourselves. The Doctrine Commission also recognized, though it did not spell out the full implications of its recognition, that what can be believed about the resurrection of Jesus must also be capable of being related to what can reasonably be believed about his ascension. The *Doctrine Report* was unanimous in its rejection of a physical ascension of Jesus:

> Whatever may have been the nature of the event underlying those narratives, and whatever its relation to the Resurrection, its physical features are to be interpreted symbolically since they are closely related to the conception of heaven as a place locally fixed beyond the sky.[8]

This is an extremely important consideration, which in terms of the coherence and interrelationship of Christian beliefs should have been explicitly brought into the discussion on Jesus' resurrection, especially since the passage acknowledges that the two beliefs are 'related'.

In the thirty years after 1938, under the influence of the 'biblical Theology' movement, there was a strong movement back to a more traditional stance. Michael Ramsey, C. F. D. Moule and a host of other scholars strongly affirmed the historicity of the empty tomb.[9] In writing my doctoral thesis against such views, I was very conscious of swimming against the stream,[10] and the vast majority of authorities cited in my first book were very much opposed to the position I sought to defend, even though there were always some scholars, such as G. W. H. Lampe, who enabled one to feel not entirely isolated![11] Now, however, the situation has radically changed, and the kind of position for which the Modernists argued is once again dominant among scholars working in this area. This can readily be illustrated by examining the four most recent collections of essays concerning the resurrection of Jesus, in which fifty-five leading authorities set out their views.[12] While there is certainly no unanimity, and scholars can still be found to defend the kind of position for which Moule argued, the dominant view, especially among those who focus on the New Testament evidence, is that what matters for contemporary scholarship is not the tradition of the empty tomb, but, rather, the evidence for the appearances of Jesus to his disciples and how it was that they came to believe that he had conquered death. This shift in scholarly opinion needs to be taken on board by the Churches, who seem in general to have moved in a reverse direction in recent years, even though the fullest and most detailed account of *The Structure of Resurrection Belief* in modern times has been written by Peter Carnley, an Anglican archbishop.[13]

One interesting finding is the comment by Stephen Davis that, in the course of all his theological reading about the resurrection in the past ten years, he has come across no scholar today who thinks of the resurrection of Jesus in terms of the resuscitation of Jesus' corpse.[14] Yet that was precisely the starting-point for mainstream Christianity for over 1,500 years, and, judging by the controversy that arose in the Church of England concerning the view of David Jenkins as bishop of Durham, it remains the view of many clergy today. In an interview with *Reader's Digest,* Archbishop George Carey affirmed that his own understanding of the resurrection was that Jesus' 'cold, dead, body, was raised alive by God',[15] so Carey might be an exception to the claim made by Davis. Carey's position, at least in this journalistic 'soundbite', sounds very similar to the literalistic understanding of the resurrection of the earliest Christian Fathers.

Etymologically, the English word *resurrection* is a translation of the Latin for 'rising again' and is used in New Testament translation for the Greek word *anastasis,* which literally means 'standing up again'. The Credal clause 'We look for the resurrection of the dead' could be more literally translated: 'We look for the standing-up-again of the corpses.' This primal meaning is present in many of the New Testament texts relating to the resurrection of Jesus. The point of the empty-tomb narratives is that the body of

Jesus was no longer there because he had been 'raised up'. We note the juxtaposition of talk of Jesus having risen from the dead with talk of the place where he had lain. We hear of his tomb being empty and the grave-clothes scattered.[16] We hear of Mary Magdalene being asked to stop clinging to Jesus, and of Thomas being invited to touch him.[17] There seems little doubt that such passages imply a concept of resurrection of a very physical and straightforward kind. This is explicitly spelt out in Luke 24: 38–43, where, faced with the disciples' apparent belief that they were seeing a spirit *pneuma*, the risen Christ is described as saying, 'Why do questionings rise in your hearts? See my hands and my feet, that it is I myself; handle me and see; for a spirit has not flesh and bones as you see that I have.' Then, finding the disciples still incredulous, Jesus asked for something to eat, and was given a piece of broiled fish which he ate in their presence to prove the actuality of his physical presence. The meaning here is consciously and unambiguously an assertion of a literal rising-up from the dead, and this is a primary source for a physicalist understanding of the resurrection of Jesus as an interpretation of what happened on the first Easter morning.

According to the fourth of the 39 Articles of the Church of England, 'Christ did truly rise again from death, and took again his body, with flesh, bones, and all things pertaining to the perfection of Man's nature; wherewith he ascended into heaven, and there sitteth.' This understanding of Jesus' resurrection was seen as having one supremely important implication for his followers: namely, that it guaranteed a like destiny for us. What happened to Jesus then would happen to us all at the end of time. The 'particles composing each individual's flesh' would be collected together, the sea would 'give up its dead', the cannibal restore the flesh he had borrowed, and 'the identical structure which death had previously destroyed would be raised to new life'.[18] This understanding of Jesus' resurrection and its implications for us was affirmed in the Apostles' Creed, with its dual assertion of the resurrection of Jesus and the resurrection of the flesh (*carnis*).

To interpret the resurrection of Jesus in so directly physical a manner necessarily raises the question of what happened subsequently to the risen body. It is no accident that Luke, who so stresses the physicality of Christ's resurrection, also goes on to assert a physical lifting-up (ascension) of Jesus' body into a localized heaven in the sky.[19] But belief in a heaven in such close proximity to this earth that a resurrected physical body could be carried there by clouds[20] is simply no longer a conceptual possibility for us. The cosmology of a 'three-decker Universe', with a hell beneath the earth, of which volcanoes are the vent-holes, and a heaven in the sky immediately above the earth, is presupposed by this picture.[21] Yet no one today can accept this cosmology. Its credibility has been totally destroyed by the rise of modern science and above all by the Copernican discoveries of the sixteenth century. Consequently, when Christians today speak of 'heaven' they locate it not in the sky, but in another dimension of being. In this new context, talk of a literal physical resurrection of Jesus simply does not fit.

The vast majority of contemporary Christians accept the need to modernize the historic understanding of what Christ's resurrection means. The most popular modification is to suggest that Jesus rose from the dead in a radically transformed kind of 'spiritual body' which was nevertheless in some sense continuous with the body laid in the tomb. Thus, C. F. D. Moule suggests: 'The material of which the body [i.e. the corpse of Jesus] was composed was somehow transformed into a different mode of existence.'[22] One ground for thinking this is that, while all the Gospel accounts report that Jesus' tomb was empty, they also suggest that there was something very unusual about Jesus' risen body. He was able to pass through locked doors, and to appear and disappear at will;[23] the disciples seem to have had difficulty in recognizing him, and when they did so they felt a sense of awe in his presence. Belief in the transformation of Jesus' body is claimed to be a way of enabling one to hold on to the empty-tomb tradition while accepting the radical differences revelealed through the appearances of Jesus. It also provides for a resurrection hope for Christians who may suppose, with St Paul in Philippians 3: 21: 'He will transfigure the body belonging to our humble state, and give it a form like that of his own resplendent body, by the power which enables him to make all things subject to himself.' At first sight it is not surprising that this understanding of the resurrection of Jesus should be endorsed by the House of Bishops of the Church of England as expressing its faith.[24]

However, there are serious logical problems with this 'half-way house'. Don Cupitt describes the concept of a 'spiritual body' as a logical hybrid, a combination of mutually incompatible terms like a 'square circle'.[25] For the resurrection body is considered to be sufficiently bodily to be seen and heard and to wear clothes, and yet at the same time to be sufficiently spiritual to pass through locked doors. How can it simultaneously possess these mutually incompatible characteristics? Consider also the question of the broiled fish. Are we to suppose that a spiritual body needs such sustenance? If it does, how can it then immediately disappear through the walls? Was the newly ingested fish instantly spiritualized so that it too could pass through the walls? It may seem crude to press such issues, but they need to be faced if one is to take the notion of a spiritual body seriously. And even if we feel able to accept that a spiritual body could itself behave in the ways required by the stories, the question of its clothes raises further problems. No one imagines that the risen Christ appeared naked to his disciples in the upper room, or to Cleopas and his companion on the road to Emmaus, or to Mary Magdalene in the garden. Yet to suppose that earthly clothes are integral to the being of a spiritual body, so that clothes and body together can appear and disappear through locked doors, is a very bizarre notion.

Another problem is that this interpretation of the spiritual body hypothesis may not harmonize with the empty-tomb traditions as easily as its defenders suppose. For if a spiritual body is designed to be the means of our embodiment in a new and glorious life in heaven, and if freedom from the limitations of earthly existence is integral to it, then the matter of which Jesus' corpse was composed should be irrelevant to it. The House of Bishops of the Church of England points out that 'our Lord's own crucified body must have undergone irreversible physiological changes very shortly after death', and therefore the bishops suggest that re-creation is a better model for the future hope than resuscitation. They add that awareness of the radical difference between the two modes of being 'helps to relate our own resurrection, where the question of an empty tomb does not arise, more intelligibly to that of Jesus'.[26] But there is an unresolved tension in this argument. The bishops rightly affirm that an integral part of the New Testament message is that Jesus' resurrection is the foundation for our future hope. But in this context an asymmetry between our corpses, which are cremated or decomposed, and Jesus' body, which was transformed and raised up, becomes serious. A spiritual body would be a better foundation for our future hope if it were not linked in people's minds to faith in the empty tomb and belief in such physical elements in the appearance stories as the accounts of Jesus eating fish. Much Easter Day preaching is vitiated by the fact that arguments in favour of the empty tomb of Jesus are used as grounds for us to have confidence in a future life, even though our tombs are supposedly to remain full. Not surprisingly, this transparent *non sequitur* destroys all confidence in the argument.

Fortunately, however, the tradition associated with belief in a physical resurrection from an empty tomb is only one of the traditions in the New Testament. St Paul is our earliest source of information as to how the resurrection of Jesus was initially understood, and it is striking that he does not once mention belief in an empty tomb. Instead Paul focuses all his attention on the appearances of Jesus. In 1 Corinthians 15 he says over and over again that Christ 'appeared' to various of the disciples and 'last of all he appeared to me'. The word translated as 'appeared' is the Greek word *ophthe*. It is the word normally used not for physical sighting, but for inner spiritual vision. It does not mean 'he was seen by'. It means 'he let himself be seen'. And the 'seeing' is always in terms of spiritual vision rather than objective sighting. Archbishop Carnley has shown that one must not push this argument too far and that some scholars have disputed it. Nevertheless, Carnley is himself clear that *ophthe* means something other than 'seeing a material object through the natural mechanism of the eye and optic nerve' and always has some connotation of a kind of seeing which is 'peculiar to religious faith'.[27]

In terms of what kind of 'seeing' the resurrection appearances were, it is significant to note that St Paul takes for granted that what happened to him on the road to Damascus was as much a resurrection appearance as any of the other of the appearances he lists. And what happened on the road to Damascus was quite explicitly an inward vision; 'God revealed his son within me' is a literal translation of Galatians 1: 15, and in Acts 26: 19 St Paul calls his experience 'a heavenly vision'. He had no doubt of its reality, even though none of his companions on the road shared in his experience. Yet this vision transformed his life. And St Paul was sure it was no resuscitated body that he saw, but rather a vision of the glory that lies ahead. For while it was a physical body that was buried, it was a spiritual body that was raised.[28]

We have already noted that many New Testament passages take a very different line from this. St Luke's understanding of the resurrection body of Jesus is ruthlessly physical, with explicit mention of 'flesh and bones', and invitations from Jesus to touch him.[29] But I suggest that this represents a later interpretation which arose partly from a wish of the disciples to insist on the 'reality' of what they had experienced, and partly because of an application to Jesus of a passage in the Psalms that says God would not allow his 'Holy One to see corruption'.[30] The first generation of Christians knew nothing of the empty-tomb stories. We know this because all early manuscripts of St Mark's Gospel end with an account of three women finding the tomb empty, followed by the statement, 'But they said nothing about this to anyone because they were afraid'.[31] This comment only makes sense if St Mark was consciously adding something hitherto unknown to the original message. St Mark would have had no need to explain such a silence if the story of the women finding Jesus' tomb empty had been part of the oral traditions about Jesus. St Mark knew he was adding something his readers had not previously been told about, and to explain this he talks of the witnesses' previous silence. The text literally says: 'No one, no anything they told.'

So there is considerable evidence that the original understanding of the resurrection of Jesus focused on his appearances, and that these appearances were initially seen as spiritual visions rather than physical sightings. In this respect it is interesting that the favoured interpretation of the appearances of Jesus by the Modernists was in terms of 'objective visions'. Major believed that it was possible that psychical research might 'provide a basis of fact' to 'render credible the substance of the New Testament resurrection narratives'.[32] One way this expectation has been fulfilled is in relation to parapsychological findings about apparitions, where we find some remarkably suggestive parallels to the New Testament data. In his work *Apparitions*, published in 1953, G. N. M. Tyrell analysed 1,684 reports of apparitions which had been investigated by the British Society for Psychical Research in the previous half-century. He stated that apparitions seemed to the percipients to be as real as something objectively seen, but that French chalk, cameras and tape-recordings never provide evidence of an apparition's presence. Apparitions sometimes appear in locked rooms, at times they vanish suddenly, at other times they fade away; they normally evade touching, and they leave no physical traces of their presence behind them; they are seen by some but not others of those present.[33] If we compare this with Jesus' appearances, we note that he appears suddenly in a locked room, he vanishes, or is slowly parted from his disciples; he is seen by some but not others of those present; he says at one time 'touch me not'.[34] These features of Jesus' appearances seem to have much more in common with reports of apparitions than with reports of objective sightings.

Investigating this phenomenon further, Canon Michael Perry, editor of the *Christian Parapsychologist*, has argued that the evidence suggests that the parapsychological phenomena of spontaneous veridical hallucinations might provide a useful analogy to the resurrection appearances of Jesus. Spontaneous veridical hallucinations are when a person 'sees' an apparition of the agent at the precise moment when the agent is undergoing some traumatic experience. 'It is an hallucination because what is seen is physically not there; it is veridical because it is observed in connection with a real event outside the percipient's normal knowledge.'[35] As well as these cases, there are reports of experimental cases where the agent caused an apparition of himself to be seen by willing it to happen. Tyrell found sixteen such cases in his survey.[36] I suggest that these findings are extremely helpful to understanding the possible nature of Jesus' appearances. They could be understood as veridical hallucinations or, perhaps better, in the Modernists' preferred terminology, 'objective visions', revealing to the minds of his disciples the fact of the survival of Jesus' spirit. The source of this vision would be Jesus himself communicating telepathically with the disciples.

This theory is supported by the consideration that telepathy is the only way a disembodied mind could communicate with an embodied one, and a veridical hallucination (more positively described as a heavenly vision!) seems the only way to explain the clothed appearance of the risen Christ. As we noted earlier, no one imagines Jesus manifesting himself naked to his disciples. Unless one is prepared to postulate 'the resurrection of Jesus' clothes', one is in real difficulties in accounting for the manner of his appearances except on the spiritual-vision hypothesis. For though one might postulate readily available gardener's clothes for the incident in the garden, one cannot make such suggestions for sudden appearances in the middle of a locked room.

The point I am making is that for many thoughtful Christians today the traditional literal physical resurrection of Jesus has become simply unthinkable: not so much because of physiological difficulties about the resuscitation of a three-day-old corpse (for to a believer God can do anything) as, more radically, because a physical resurrection requires a physical ascension, and a physical ascension requires a 'three-decker Universe', with a literal heaven in the sky immediately above the earth. But this picture is incompatible with the experience of jet travel, quite apart from everything else we have learned in the past four centuries about the nature of reality. Hence, for many the traditional interpretation of Jesus' resurrection has become literally unthinkable. At this point, however, parapsychological research can become of immense importance to Christian belief, for it provides a way of making sense of the stories of Jesus' appearances which accords with other well-documented cases, and which may also be closer to the way the resurrection of Jesus was understood by the very first disciples.

One great advantage of the parapsychological interpretation of the nature of Jesus' resurrection is that it makes it relevant to the lives of ordinary believers. When I was a parish priest in Birmingham I was very struck to discover that by far the most common ground for belief in a future life among my parishioners was that many seem to have had some momentary visionary experience or sense of the awareness of a deceased loved one which had convinced them that 'all was well'. Douglas Davies has recently found that 35 per cent of people have had such an experience, and it is particularly common among bereaved people. The experience is reported as very positive and reinforces ideas of an afterlife among those who have it.[37] Jesus' appearances would thus be a particularly vivid, full and well-documented instance of a phenomenon well known to parapsychological researchers.[38] Hick points out that a sense that a loved person who has recently died is 'invisibly present comforting, guiding or challenging' is widely reported. He suggests that 'this may also have been true of Jesus in the days and weeks after his death'.[39] To avoid any misunderstanding, I would stress that I am not here discussing the claims of spiritualists to be able to contact the dead through mediums, and I have shown elsewhere that there are very serious difficulties in the way of taking such reports seriously.[40] The parallel I am drawing is with the widespread contemporary experience of a bereaved person sensing the living presence of a deceased person and being convinced by that experience that 'all is well' and that there is indeed life after death. On this understanding, the experience of the risen Christ is a raising to the nth degree of an experience which in a far less vivid form is in fact a very common human phenomenon.

Many people object to such comparisons, arguing that the resurrection of Jesus is wholly different in kind from any other event in history. For Wolfhart Pannenberg 'Jesus' resurrection is the basis for the perception of his divinity'.[41] A similar view is expressed by James Dunn, who states that 'the resurrection of Jesus' was 'a fundamental part of the cause' of 'Jesus being spoken of in divine terms'.[42] In the previous chapter I showed grounds for questioning this way of thinking on the basis of what we mean by attributing divinity to Jesus. At this point I question it on the quite different ground that it would empty the resurrection of Jesus of all significance to the rest of humanity if it were thought in principle to be wholly unique to him and a consequence of his divinity. St Paul's perspective was entirely different. For him the credibility of the proclamation of Jesus' resurrection depended entirely on supposing that what happened to him was similar in kind to what happens to all human beings:

> If there is no resurrection of the dead, then Christ has not been raised; if Christ has not been raised, our preaching is in vain and your faith is in vain. We are even found to be misrepresenting God, because we testified of God that he raised Christ, whom he did not raise if it is true that the dead are not raised. For if the dead are not raised, then Christ has not been raised [43]

The historical importance of Jesus' resurrection appearances lies in the fact that they were so utterly convincing to those who experienced them. Because of this sense of certainty the Christian hope for a future life after the death of the physical body came into being. This understanding of Jesus' resurrection and its significance is clearly expressed in the first letter of St Peter where we read that 'in the body he (Jesus) was put to death; in the spirit he was brought to life'. Because of this, his disciples felt themselves 'born anew to a living hope' and could expect of the dead that 'although in the body they received the sentence common to all men, they might in the spirit be alive with the life of God'.[44]

Unfortunately, this original spiritual understanding was superseded by a ruthlessly physical doctrine of the resurrection of the flesh which from the second to the seventeenth century dominated Christian thinking. What is clear, however, is that almost all thinking Christians now accept that a literal reconstitution of the buried or cremated corpse is no longer credible. The international consultation on English texts has wisely left talk of 'resurrection' in the obscurity of the transliterated Latin word. Congregations would jib at saying, 'we look forward to the standing-up again of the corpses', or to 'the rising again of the flesh', even though that is what the Nicene and Apostles' Creeds respectively say. The problem is that once one tries to spell out what a literal physical resurrection would actually be like, where it might be located and what social conditions might obtain there, one rapidly finds oneself piling absurdity upon absurdity.[45] Apart from Jehovah's Witnesses' tracts, I know of no contemporary book that spells out such a position. Almost all contemporary Christians use the word 'resurrection' to mean that our personalities will be given new and quite different 'spiritual bodies' to serve as vehicles for our self-expression and development in heaven. The only bond of union between our present and future bodies is that they will be 'owned' successively by the same personality. This is the view adopted by the Church of England Doctrine Commission in 1938 and by the Catholic bishops of Holland in their 1965 Catechism.[46] It is the view implicit in any understanding of resurrection which distances itself from belief in the resuscitation of the buried or cremated corpse and which stresses the transformation and glory of the life to come. The Modernist claim is that, if the resurrection of Jesus is to contribute in any way to our understanding of what we may expect after death, then we must regain that spiritual understanding of Jesus' resurrection which both St Paul and the author of the first Letter of Peter saw as its true significance.

9

Modernist and contemporary views of life after death

We saw in the last chapter that what underpinned the Modernists' concern for a spiritual understanding of the resurrection of Jesus was their total commitment to belief in personal immortality. It was vital to them that what was proclaimed in relation to Jesus could also be proclaimed in relation to our own future hope. Hence, they resisted any account of Jesus' resurrection which made it wholly unlike what we can realistically hope for as our own future destiny. They also argued strenuously for belief in the immortality of the soul, which they saw as an integral part of any realistic faith. Paul Edwards describes how in 1922 Kirsopp Lake, in his book *Immortality and the Modern Mind*, urged the Church to replace belief in the resurrection of the body by belief in the survival of the disembodied mind, and how he provided in an appendix an account of all previous efforts to excise 'resurrection of the flesh' from the Apostles' Creed.[1] This went further than most Modernists felt necessary. Most were willing to continue to use the term 'resurrection' as long as it was clearly understood that what was being talked of was a 'spiritual body' suitable for a wholly different mode of existence, and not the 'resurrection of the flesh' understood in a totally physical manner as implied by some defenders of the empty-tomb tradition. In general, however, Modernists preferred to place greater emphasis on the immortality of the soul; and Dean Inge, as president of the MCU from 1924 to 1934, urged the importance of a more spiritual and Platonic understanding of eternal life in God.[2]

The Modernists achieved the most significant recognition of their position in the statement on 'Resurrection' in the report of the Doctrine Commission in 1938, which said:

> We ought to reject quite frankly the literalistic belief in a future resuscitation of the actual physical frame which is laid in the

tomb, it is to be affirmed none the less, that in the life of the world to come the soul or spirit will still have its appropriate organ of expression and activity, which is one with the body of earthly life in the sense that it bears the same relation to the same spiritual entity. What is important when we are speaking of the identity of any person's 'body' is not its physico-chemical constitution, but its relation to that person.[3]

What this report does is to accept the view that personhood is to be identified with the 'soul or spirit' rather than with a 'physico-chemical constitution', and that in the life of the world to come people will receive an embodiment which is quite other than the physical frame laid in the tomb. They also noted that if empirical evidence were to be forthcoming which could show that the mind could survive the dissolution of the body, this would remove 'an obstacle to the acceptance of the Christian doctrine of eternal life'. However, they felt such empirical research was likely to have limited usefulness since on principle it could disclose nothing about the quality of the resurrection life or of fellowship with God within it.

However, as with what the *Doctrine Report* said about the resurrection of Jesus, the 1938 publication marked a high spot in the acceptance of Modernist views. Thereafter, for the next two generations, the emphasis has swung back to a renewed stress on the language of bodily resurrection and a turning-away from talk of the soul or spirit.

According to the very influential biblical scholar Oscar Cullman, 'Christian resurrection faith is irreconcilable with the Greek concept of the immortality of the soul.'[4] In common with other writers of the 'Biblical Theology' movement, Cullman argued that belief in the immortality of the soul should be dismissed as an alien Hellenistic intrusion into the pure Hebrew concept of man as a psychosomatic unity whose future hope depends wholly on the belief in supernatural restoration of his total embodiment. The background to this view is the fact that early Judaism unequivocally identified personhood with physical embodiment, and that this doctrine is in stark contrast with Plato's view that the person is the soul. It is common to hold that this Hebrew understanding of man lies behind the New Testament teaching and explains why the New Testament argues for bodily resurrection as essential for us since God 'alone has immortality'.[5] The strongest evidence in support of this view is the fact that all four Gospels present the resurrection of Jesus in fairly straightforward physical terms, and in every case report the emptiness of his tomb as evidence for his actual 'uprising'.

But there are a number of problems with this view. First, it is historically the case that the initial sharp contrast between Hebrew and Greek ways of thought did not endure. It is quite easy to show that in later Judaism the soul could be regarded as distinct from the body, and that this change in Jewish thought was not necessarily derived from Greek philosophy but emerged naturally from within Judaism as Jewish thinkers began to follow up and explore the implications of their developing belief in the possibility of a life after death.[6] And when the New Testament is approached without the presupposition that its authors held the same views as their distant ancestors, it at once becomes apparent that a wide variety of opinion about the nature of man can be discerned in the New Testament, and even in the writings of individual authors. St Paul in particular is thoroughly inconsistent in his anthropology. Thus, in 2 Corinthians 5 he cannot decide whether he expects his new 'spiritual body' to be put on over his existing one or whether the future life will require him 'to leave his home in the body' altogether. He asserts both ideas with equal confidence in almost successive verses. And with regard to the resurrection of Jesus, we saw in the last chapter that there are serious grounds for believing that St Paul knew nothing of the empty-tomb tradition. Certainly his denial that flesh and blood could ever inherit the Kingdom of God[7] seems hard to reconcile with any kind of belief that Jesus' flesh and blood had already done so!

Hence, it is altogether too simplistic to describe New Testament theology as working solely within the anthropology of ancient Judaism, or to insist that the only understanding of Jesus' resurrection that is possible is one that requires the restoration of the same psychosomatic entity as had existed previously. And when this line of reasoning is extended to the Christian hope in general, yet further problems arise. For if the concept of the soul were indeed to be excluded in favour of the ancient Hebraic identification of personhood with the existing physical embodiment, then it ceases to be possible to talk in terms of radical transformation. For the whole point of identifying persons with their bodies is lost if 'different', 'changed' or 'spiritual' bodies are to be postulated for our supposed future life.

A truly psychosomatic account of human personhood insists that 'man is a physical and psychical whole which consists of a complex of parts, each part being at the same time physiological and psychical in itself'.[8] Precisely this view is presented in the Old Testament, in which heart, kidneys, bowels, liver, inward parts, flesh and bones are all explicitly mentioned as shaping and determining our present character and emotions.[9] It was for this very reason that the ancient Hebrews did not at first even consider the possibility of life after death, for they believed a human's only possible real life was on this earth and depended wholly on the continuing in being of his or her personal embodiment. This is why when the idea of a fully personal future life first emerged during the Maccabean persecution, it was expressed in terms of a literal resurrection of precisely the body that was martyred,[10] for only such a resurrection could ensure personal continuance. Later, when serious reflection took place on the likelihood of such a resurrection occurring, the older anthropology came be questioned, and a move towards a dualist understanding began to take place.

Precisely the same process took place among the early Christians. From the second century onwards an extremely literal understanding dominated much Western Christian thinking, and the doctrine of the resurrection of the flesh emerged as orthodoxy. Then, as Christians became conscious of the difficulties in such an account, their anthropology moved again in the direction of Platonism. The problem with seeking to go back to an earlier Hebraism in the twentieth century is that it would entail either that one abandon belief in a future life or that one accept an utterly literal picture of it. When twentieth-century Christians have pondered on these issues almost all have come to acknowledge the impossibility of returning to the original creeds. Thus, although the Biblical Theology movement has encouraged some theologians to prefer talk of 'resurrection' to talk of 'immortality' we find that when we clarify what they actually mean by 'resurrection' it is clear that there has been no real return to the older ways of thinking.

I know of no contemporary scholar of any denomination who believes in what the authors of the Apostles' Creed wished to affirm concerning the *resurrectionem carnis*. Their ideas have vanished so completely from our contemporary consciousness that most Christians have no idea that the Creed affirmed any such thing. Indeed, Robert Morgan, a university lecturer at Oxford, thinks that the Apostles' Creed 'rightly abandoned' the old Roman Creed's 'resurrection of the flesh' and adopted St Paul's language of 'the body that shall be'.[11] In fact the authors of the Apostles' Creed believed exactly what Rufinus, Athenagoras, Tertullian, Irenaeus, Jerome and all the rest of the early Fathers believed about the essential importance of exactly the same particles being reassembled in order for resurrection to be intelligible.[12] We owe the replacement of 'flesh' by 'body' to a deliberate decision by Cranmer to alter the Christian affirmation over a thousand years later. And since the *Alternative Service Book* of 1980 has removed the last vestiges of the earlier translations from the Baptismal services, and since undergraduate theologians no longer read the Fathers or study the Creeds in their original language, the old controversies about whether to affirm fleshly resurrection no longer exist.

Thus, when Christian leaders today talk of resurrection, what they almost invariably mean is that after death *we* receive new and quite different bodies to serve as vehicles for our self-expression and development in heaven. And the only bond of union between our present and future bodies is that they are 'owned' successively by the same personality. This understanding of resurrection raises no insuperable practical difficulties, because modern physics allows for the theoretical possibility of plural spaces in no spatial relationship whatever to each other, provided that each is subject to entirely different physical laws. Hence, one can postulate that the resurrection world (heaven) exists in another space and provides a wholly new kind of environment for further development and advance. This would tie in with St Paul's view that heaven transcends all that we can visualize or expect: 'things beyond our seeing, things beyond our hearing, things beyond our imagining, all prepared by God for those who love him'.[13]

It is not always appreciated, however, by the many writers who embrace this understanding of resurrection that it depends absolutely on the validity of the concept of the soul. It is a necessary part of the hypothesis that the point of contact between the two worlds cannot be physical. If, therefore, *I* am to exist in this heaven in another space, it follows that what is meant by the word *I* cannot be exhaustively confined to my present embodiment. This is implicitly recognized by many writers, who describe what ensures continuity between the two worlds in terms such as 'the person', 'the essential part of what we are', 'the vital principle of our being', 'the pattern of what we are', or 'our moral and intellectual qualities'. The irony is that these phrases, used by many writers who often claim not to believe in the soul, happen to be the meaning that the *Concise Oxford Dictionary* gives to the word *soul*. So, though many deny the word, they find themselves compelled to affirm everything that the word actually means, for without some notion of a non-material principle of continuity, no wholly other mode of existence in heaven can be postulated.

In 1996 the Church of England Doctrine Commission tried to wrestle with these problems in a new way in its report on *The Mystery of Salvation*. What it sought to do was to formulate a fresh way forward which would reconcile belief in the 'psychosomatic understanding of human nature' with an understanding of salvation which would be compatible with it. It argued that

> it would not be possible to speak of salvation in terms of the destiny of souls after death, if the soul is thought of as the detachable spiritual part of ourselves. If the essential human being is an embodied whole, our ultimate destiny must be the resurrection and transformation of our entire being.

It claims that 'to speak thus is not to abandon talk of the soul but to seek its redefinition'. What the word is needed for is

> to represent the essential nature which constitutes us in our individual particularities. That essence of humanity is certainly not the matter of the body, for that is continuously changing through wear and tear, eating and drinking. What provides continuity and unity through that flux of change is not material but [in a vague but suggestive phrase] the vastly complex information-bearing pattern in which that material is organised. That pattern can surely be considered the carrier of memories and of personality.[14]

What happens at death, according to this theory, is that death 'dissolves the embodiment of that pattern, but the person whose that pattern is, is "remembered" by God, who in love holds that unique being in his care'. However, there must at some point be a 'fuller realisation of God's purpose for us all'. This will come with 'the resurrection of the body'. The Doctrine Commission in 1996 was as convinced as its predecessor in 1938 that 'it is not to be supposed that the material of the resurrected body is the same as that of the old ... St Paul warned us that "flesh and blood cannot inherit the kingdom of God, nor does the perishable inherit the imperishable".' The Commission suggests that St Paul's expression, 'a spiritual body' 'does not mean "a body consisting of spirit" but "a body animated by the Holy Spirit". The only clue we have to this bodily reality is the glorified body of the Risen Lord.'[15]

The premiss on which the 1996 report is written is that biblical studies, philosophy of mind, and modern science are all moving inexorably towards a psychosomatic understanding of what it means to be human and that Christian theology must adapt to this. There is very great force in this argument, especially for anyone who holds to the characteristic Modernist position on the unity of the sciences and the need for our thinking about religious matters to be in tune with the rest of our understanding. But there are significant theological, philosophical and scientific objections to the presuppositions outlined here.

First, from the point of view of the doctrine of God it is very problematic to assume this position. The Commission is, of course, right that many philosophers today reject the concept of the soul, but what this overlooks is that for the very same reasons such philosophers also reject belief in God. As Antony Kenny points out, 'most philosophers find immateriality problematic', and if anything the difficulties are greater with belief in God, 'a non-embodied mind active throughout the universe',[16] than with the soul. If one is going to make majority secular opinion determinative for faith, one cannot pick and choose thus, and certainly not between two concepts of the same logical status.

The second problem arises in comparing the relative intellectual acceptability of resurrection of the body as against immortality of the soul. The point is that the intellectual difficulties that the Commission acknowledges as facing belief in the soul pale into utter insignificance compared with the intellectual difficulties involved in explicating a belief in resurrection; about these the

Commission is totally silent. In addition to the problems the two doctrines share, such as how to establish continuity of identity through such a change, there are the mind-boggling difficulties entailed in spelling out what resurrection might actually be like in practice. I tried to do this in *Christian Beliefs about Life after Death*, and compared to the problems encountered there *Immortality or Extinction?* was very easy to write. Having taught both subjects over the last twenty-five years, I have to say that, whereas lectures relating to the soul always attract lively discussion, any attempt to interest people in bodily resurrection goes down like a stone. The doctrine is simply perceived as a non-starter. Likewise, while television documentaries on immortality are of constant interest, I cannot recall resurrection being discussed at all except in relation to Jesus. These observations can be backed up statistically by the findings of Professor Douglas Davies in his article 'Contemporary belief in life after death'. Davies interviewed 1,603 individuals at length about their views about what happens after death. The results were:

Nothing happens, we come to the end of life	29 per cent
Our soul passes on to another world	34 per cent
Our bodies await a resurrection	8 per cent
We come back as something or someone else	12 per cent
Trust in God, all is in God's hands	22 per cent

In addition, the soul was the most often selected second option among those who gave two responses. So '54 individuals linked the soul with "trust in God", 26 linked it with "coming back as something else" and 21 with resurrection'. Moreover, 42 individuals combined three choices, 'trusting God, soul and resurrection'. So in every respect it was the dominant option. It is also interesting to note that 18 per cent of atheists and 15 per cent of agnostics believe in the soul while only 2 per cent of either believe in the resurrection. Similarly noteworthy is that only 4 per cent of Anglicans asked affirmed a belief in resurrection, and no Methodists in this group mentioned it. That is particularly interesting in view of the heavy emphasis on the resurrection in the Churches' liturgies and preaching.[17]

Further problems face *The Mystery of Salvation*'s proposals for the mode of the future resurrection: namely, that after death we

shall live on in God's memory until God creates again the infor-
mation-bearing pattern in which our identity is preserved. The
first part of this schema suffers exactly the same defects as when
it was originally proposed by Charles Hartshorne that 'we will
live on in the complete and infallible memory of God'. The
problem with this view is that there is all the difference in the
world between actually living on and simply being remembered.
John Hick pointed out very tellingly that Hartshorne 'gives the
seriously misleading impression that the state of being remembered constitutes as full and real existence as the state of being
alive. But this is manifestly false.'[18]

The second part of the schema is equally flawed for the same
reason as the endlessly discussed 'replica schema' of Hick (which
he no longer actively defends).[19] The basic problem is that,
although God could certainly create the same information-
bearing pattern as I am now, and although that information-
bearing pattern (carrying my memories and my personality)
would certainly think he was me and be recognized by others as
me, he would not actually *be* me. To explain why not, let us
suppose that, instead of waiting for my death God were to create
a duplicate of me now carrying exactly the same memories and
personality. Confronted with my duplicate I would conclude God
had cloned me completely, but never for one minute would I
regard my duplicate as other than a new-found identical twin, and
my death would still entail the end of my consciousness, even if a
duplicate consciousness were created again at a later date.

I conclude that the proposals in *The Mystery of Salvation* fail to
provide for any adequate possibility of continued personal identity
and I argue that the *sine qua non* for any new life, whether in a
disembodied or a resurrected state, continues to require the continuity of my soul through death. This need continues to be recognized by the Roman Catholic Church. According to Pope John Paul
II's encyclical *Man's Condition after Death,* 'The Church affirms
that a spiritual element survives and subsists after death, an
element endowed with consciousness and will, so that the "human
self" subsists, though deprived for the present of the complement of
its body.'[20] *The Catechism of the Catholic Church* affirms that the
soul 'is immortal: it does not perish when it separates from the body
at death'. In death 'the human body decays and the soul goes to
meet God, while awaiting its reunion with its glorified body'.[21]

I suggest that, despite the problems to which *The Mystery of Salvation* refers, it is possible to continue to defend the concept of the soul. Many reject soul–body dualism because of all that modern science has shown us about the intimate relationship that exists between all our thinking, feeling and willing and some quite specific brain states. But there is no reason for them to do so, since the same facts can all be equally be explained by a doctrine of mind–brain interaction which can also go to explain further facts about how the mind in turn can affect the brain. Richard Swinburne believes that dualism is 'inescapable' if we are really to explain human existence and experience.[22] First he points out that, though 'the mental life of thought, sensation and purpose may be caused by physico-chemical events in the brain, it is quite different from those events'. Second, he draws attention to the fact that 'conscious experiences are causally efficacious. Our thoughts and feelings are not just phenomena caused by goings-on in the brain; they cause other thoughts and feelings and they make a difference to the agent's behaviour.' Third, he suggests that 'though a human soul has a structure and character which is formed in part through the brain to which it is connected ... [it] ... acquires some independence of that brain.'[23] Keith Ward adopts the same position: 'Of course the soul depends on the brain ... but the soul need not always depend on the brain, any more than a man need always depend on the womb which supported his life before birth.'[24]

On this hypothesis the soul is an emergent property that comes into existence in the course of life. Throughout life it interacts with the body, but in principle it is separable from it, and perhaps at death separation may occur. This hypothesis appears to be supported by the claims made by many resuscitated persons that at the moment their hearts stopped beating they found themselves outside their bodies looking down with interest on the attempts made by the medical teams to revive them. What makes these claims evidential is that their observations seem to be extraordinarily accurate and to accord with what would have been seen if they genuinely were looking down from above.[25]

A second supporting argument for the emergence of the human soul is the view that rational thought, scientific inquiry and responsible decision-making all depend on the view that human persons are genuinely free agents. A materialist understanding of the mind threatens that freedom because the human brain is a physical organism, and as such is subject to the laws of physics and chemistry. One such law is that physical causes always precede physical effects, and hence teleological kinds of explanation (i.e. explaining natural phenomena by reference to future goals) are inappropriate. But almost all human researchers think of their own work as responsible and goal-directed, and a person presenting a rational argument thinks that he or she is doing something more than simply giving a report on his or her own past brain states. When Jacques Monod declared that his goal in writing *Chance and Necessity* was to show that there was no such thing as purpose, his argument depended on exempting himself from its remit.[26]

A third argument for the immortality of the human soul is the claim that human beings can enter into a relationship of love and fellowship with God, and that God will wish to sustain this relationship through death. The evidence of prayer and worship is that experiential knowledge of God is central to living faith. Yet God is not apprehended through the senses; so if the divine–human encounter is real, it must be that God makes the reality of his presence felt other than through neural pathways: direct to the mind, and not *via* sensory stimuli. This can only happen if the soul exists as a substantive reality.[27]

A similar but secular argument is derived from telepathy, by which I mean the transfer of information from one mind to another mind without the use of the neural pathways of the brain. Concerning its intellectual validity let me simply quote the judgement of Professor Eysenck in 1960:

> Unless there is a gigantic conspiracy involving some thirty University departments all over the world and several hundred respected scientists in various fields, many of them originally hostile to the claims of the psychical researchers, the only conclusion an unbiased observer can come to must be that there does exist a small body of people who obtain knowledge existing in other people's minds by means as yet unknown to science.[28]

It is certainly striking that most who have attended to the evidence seem now to be convinced that telepathy is a reality. Moreover, with every year that passes the case appears to grow stronger as more instances are reported and earlier reports are vindicated. The relevance of this to our present discussion was best expressed by Keith Campbell:

> Parapsychological phenomena, by definition, demonstrate capacities of mind which exceed any capacities of brain. The brain is receptive only to information that arrives by neural pathways and so is confined to perception by way of the senses ... If some people are receptive to the contents of the minds of another by some more direct means such as telepathy then those minds are just not brains.[29]

That argument seems to me unanswerable, and Campbell left a notable hostage to fortune when he developed it, in the light of the evidence for telepathy now available.

The grounds for believing in the reality of the human soul are therefore the experience of separation from the body near the point of death, the experience of reflective rational thought, the experience of divine human encounter in ways that transcend the physical, and the existence of paranormal experiences. We have grounds for thinking that these are real human experiences and therefore at least some grounds for believing the soul to be a reality in this life. Whether there are sufficient grounds to say more we must leave till the next chapter.

10

Modern religious experiencing

From the very beginning, modern theology has highlighted the importance of religious experience to living faith. Friedrich Schleiermacher was hailed as the 'father of modern theology' for his new way of approaching the subject-matter with which theology deals. He constantly insisted that ultimate authority lay not in the doctrinal formularies of the past and not in any sacred writings, but in the religious experience itself, 'in which all other activities are set aside and the whole soul is dissolved in the immediate feeling of the infinite and eternal'.[1] He insisted that 'all truly religious characters have had a mystical trait', and he urged that in the end all theological dogmas were to be tested against the religious experiencing of the contemporary Christian community, Similarly, in Britain almost all the leaders of the Broad Church movement in the nineteenth century referred to Samuel Taylor Coleridge as their spiritual father, and he likewise insisted that the only 'evidences of Christianity' worth having were when a person felt the need of it and found it to be true in life. According to James Livingston, 'Coleridge with Schleiermacher founded modern theological apologetics on a new basis, human experience.'[2] They were enabled to criticize past dogmas of the Church and query the authority of biblical texts because their own faith was based directly on their own experiencing of God.

This new approach was crucial to the Broad Church movement. For example, Rowland Williams defended the right to practice biblical criticism by arguing that the Bible was the 'written voice of the congregation' deriving from human experience, and he therefore rejected the 'fiction of an external revelation'. In the area of doctrine, he argued that justification by faith should be understood as 'the peace of mind or sense of divine approval which comes of trust in a righteous God, rather than a fiction of merit by transfer'. Similarly, redemption should be understood as 'salvation from evil through sharing the Saviour's spirit' rather than as 'a notion of purchase from God through the price of his bodily pains'.[3] It was for such sentiments that he was brought to trial for heresy before the Judicial Committee of the Privy Council, and his acquittal in 1864 was the turning-point in the acceptance of the legitimacy of biblical and doctrinal criticism within the university system.

The Modernists likewise constantly appealed to living contemporary experience as a ground to challenge beliefs which they believed to be outmoded. For example, Percy Gardner, president of the MCU from 1917 to 1922, urged that 'religious beliefs, like all the active principles of our lives, can only be justified when they are based on realities and experience ... True doctrine seems to me definable as that which accords with the essential facts of man's spiritual surroundings.'[4] Similarly, in 1904, in a presidential address to the MCU on 'The Task of Liberal Theology', Douglas Morrison urged the need 'to emancipate the facts of the Christian faith from the mists of theory ... and announce the great fundamental truth that the Christian religion is not a theory but a profound, transforming, ethical and religious experience'.[5] Both Hastings Rashdall and Dean Inge constantly also appealed to experience. The *Logos* doctrine was a living reality to them because they had felt it at work in their lives. Inge urged that Christianity must have a mystical element in it. Without 'the feeling of immediate communion with God ... we shall have a dead Church'. At a time when the authority of both Bible and Church are questioned, faith needs the reinforcements which 'can only come for the depths of the religious consciousness itself'.[6]

This whole approach to theology was, of course, fiercely attacked by the rise to dominance of Barthian Neo-orthodoxy, which revived an insistence on revelation alone as the source of faith. This stress on revelation was also encouraged in a much milder manner in Britain by the Biblical Theology movement. Likewise, both Anglo-Catholic and Evangelical traditions, though certainly seeking to encourage religious feelings, always urge that these follow the prescribed pattern of their respective traditions. Consequently for two generations religious experiencing tended to be soft-pedalled by the dominant schools of theology in mid-twentieth-century Britain.

Now, however, religious experiencing has come very much back to the centre of the theological scene, just as it was in the palmy days of the Modernists' greatest influence. In particular, religious experiencing is at the centre of contemporary philosophy of religion, because there is widespread agreement that it is impossible to prove God's existence by arguments that all rational persons should accept. We appear to be living in an ambiguous world which can be interpreted theistically or atheistically, as shown by the fact that equally reasonable, well-informed and sensitive thinkers do come to opposing viewpoints on this issue. Christian philosophers, such as Basil Mitchell or Richard Swinburne, who wish to provide a justification for religious belief, or to argue for the coherence of theism, suggest that it is possible to construct a cumulative rational case for belief in the existence of God, as one way of making sense of the way the world is.[7] They then suggest that for the believer the additional personal knowledge which comes from religious experiencing may tip the balance of probability in favour of belief. A similar consideration may be at work in the attitude towards religious faith of the various scientists whose views we discussed in chapter 5. We noted there that for Stephen Hawking 'physics suggests the possibility of a mathematical God, but not a being with whom one can have a personal relationship'.[8] By contrast, John Polkinghorne believes in a personal God because, in addition to the knowledge he has acquired through modern physics, he also believes in the reality of religious experiencing.[9]

This mode of arguing corresponds well to the intuitions of the average religious believer today, who accepts that faith does not lie on the same level of certainty as scientific knowledge, and who tends to appeal to personal experience as grounds for continuing with the life of faith. But this whole approach depends on supposing that religious experiencing provides additional grounds for belief, and that it is appropriate for Christian theology to make appeal to such data. It also depends on supposing that when a Christian claims to have a sense of the presence of God, the nature of the experience and what flows from it are such as to encourage a view that God was indeed its source. It presupposes also that God, who cannot be discerned by any of our five senses, can nevertheless be thought of as being 'encountered'. All these presuppositions are disputable and have been challenged.

The first problem is whether religious experiencing is rightly understood as providing the believer with any additional grounds for faith. This is explicitly denied by Nicholas Lash, who argues:

> It is simply a mistake to infer that . . . accounts of experience of God constitute some peculiar, untestable and incommunicable 'religious addition' to a general, universally accessible account of what human beings suffer, remember, hope, fear, achieve and undergo.[10]

Lash persuasively argues that God can be known through the ordinary, and is not confined to that minority who claim unusual private experiences or states of mind. I would not contest this. My only concern is to argue that it remains the case that many do base their own claim to knowledge of God on experiences which transcend the general experiences of common life, and that the evidential character of such claims is crucial to understanding them.

It is true that much that can be described as 'religious experiencing' constitutes a way of looking at the everyday world. John Hick's article 'Religious faith as experiencing-as' gives a very good account of how much of faith can be understood as a different way of experiencing natural phenomena. On this view, atheists and believers confront the same realities, but the one interprets them religiously and the other naturalistically.[11] However, it seems to me crucial not to limit discussion of religious experiencing to this kind of experience alone, but also to consider the form of religious experiencing in which 'the mystic's mind is being directly affected by the divine reality', as Hick explores in his essay on 'Religious experience: its nature and vitality'.[12]

Richard Swinburne argues in his essay on 'The evidential value of religious experience' that there are five ways of using the expression 'religious experience'. In the first two senses, God is perceived through taking public phenomena religiously; in the other three usages of the term, 'the divine is apprehended through something private to the subject'.[13] It is important to be aware of these differences of usage. I am here focusing on the latter and looking at the evidential value of claims to apprehend or be conscious of a 'dynamic external presence' (to use Ninian Smart's definition of a numinous experience).[14] It seems to me that this is what people normally mean when they say they have had a religious experience. And I very much agree with the view so ably defended in Caroline Franks Davis's *The Evidential Force of Religious Experience* that we should normally adopt a *descriptive*, rather than a *prescriptive* use of language.[15] People who report theistic religious experiences think they are conscious of a presence beyond themselves. If we reinterpet or demythologize what they are saying and suggest with T. R. Miles that what they 'really' mean is something quite other than this, we are imposing an alien or 'hetero-interpretation' upon them, and this is to bias our inquiry and beg the questions we are discussing.[16] In other words, unless we have grounds for repudiating their perspective we should treat them as being what they claim to be.

Hick argued in his essay 'Rational theistic belief without proofs' that for the major figures in the Christian tradition, as for the Old Testament prophets, 'awareness of God was so vivid that ... they could no more help believing in the reality of God than in the reality of the material world and of their human neighbours ... God was known to the prophets and apostles as a dynamic will interacting with their own wills; a sheerly given personal reality.'[17] Hick correctly argues that for such persons belief in God was rational. We can also add to Hick's examples people from other traditions, such as Muhammad or Zoroaster, and especially theistic Hindu worshippers, whose tradition explicitly regards the divine as more real than the external world.

However, there is an objection to seeing this kind of approach as evidential, and that is that compelling religious experiences of this type are relatively rare, whereas perceptual experience of the external world is universal. Why should we not regard this small minority as suffering from delusions about their experiences – like, perhaps, the paranoiac who constantly hears threats against him, or the alcoholic who sees green snakes, or the schizophrenic who sees hallucinations or hears voices?

But there are good reasons for us not to lump all these classes together. The reason we do not accept the hallucinations of the mentally disturbed as evidential is because they show in other ways that they are not attuned to reality. By contrast, the primary religious figures were manifestly in touch with reality. What is impressive about the prophets is the soundness of their political and social judgements. On any reckoning, Jesus of Nazareth was at the very least a wise and perceptive teacher, and Muhammad was a brilliant general, statesman and lawgiver. Likewise, contemporary religious experience is associated with a high level of mental alertness and psychological stability. David Hay's research shows that religious experience is reported by 65 per cent of postgraduates, by 56 per cent of those educated beyond the age 20, but by only 29 per cent of those who left school at 15. It is also reported by 49 per cent of people in the professions, but by only 32 per cent of unskilled workers.[18] People who have religious experience are also likely to be happier and better adjusted psychologically.[19] Hence, to identify either prophetic or contemporary religious experience with mental disorder would seem wholly unjustified.

There is nevertheless a problem with some personality types and with some over-intense religious groups. The problems arise in particular in cases where religious experiencing is routinely expected of people, for this can lead to that kind of auto-induced euphoria that led Immanuel Kant to suspect all religious experiencing.[20] It also led Albrecht Ritschl to his damning judgements in *The History of Pietism*. As E. C. Moore puts it, 'What impressed his sane mind was the fact that unhealthy minds have often claimed as their revelation from God, an experience which might with more truth be assigned to almost any other source.'[21] Today this phenomena is at its most perplexing among adherents of new religious movements whose systems of belief lack any kind of philosophical or theological plausibility, and yet often lead to sincere religious feeling and in some cases to radical change of life.

Given these problems, it seems that the 'interpretation of religion' that has the best chance of according with reality is that provided John Hick. On his view, human beings do encounter transcendent reality, but their response to it is always mediated through the religious, cultural and scientific world-view in which they live.[22] Moreover, Richard Swinburne is right to advise 'more than normal scepticism' when a subject claims that 'God has called him to do something . . . for there is a natural tendency of many men to believe that others, and so a fortiori God, wish them to do what they want to do anyway'.[23]

However, though God may speak through the normal human consciousness, the evidential character of religious experiencing depends on believing that human consciousness is not its ultimate source. When people report a 'sense of the presence of God' or an awareness of an ultimate reality, they normally feel it wholly false to their experience to be told that it is simply self-generated, rather than a response to transcendent reality. In discussing Don Cupitt earlier, we highlighted the concern felt by both Muhammad and St Anselm lest the object of their worship might be no more than a product of their own imagination. Hence, we noted what a relief it had been to Anselm to have had an experience so profound that all doubts vanished.

Christian saints and mystics of East and West unite in insisting that their religious experiencing provide them with what Eric Mascall describes as 'an experimental awareness of God ... which is not mediated by the senses'.[24] Yet if our senses give us no direct knowledge of God, how can we possibly have that immediate awareness which is essential to the saint's moment of vision. For St Paul it was axiomatic that 'spiritual things are spiritually discerned'.[25] Swinburne talks of experiences being mediated by a 'sixth sense' and suggests that many mystics talk of encountering God *via* 'nothingness' or 'darkness' to make the point that their experience of God was 'not mediated via any sensations'.[26] Hick suggests that 'when the mystic's mind is being directly affected by the divine reality', a partial analogy for what is happening might be found 'in the kind of mental impact of one human mind on another that is called telepathy'.[27] What lies behind all these claims is the conviction that people really do 'encounter' the divine reality, even though the five senses are not involved in this. But if the human mind can have access to knowledge otherwise than through the neural pathways leading from the senses to the brain, then a dualist theory of mind–brain is required.

As we saw in the previous chapter, this raises problems for the philosophy of religion, because it ties belief in the evidential value of religious experiencing to a theory in the philosophy of mind which has been increasingly questioned by mainstream philosophy. But what is the alternative? If we suggest that the 'goings-on in my brain' responsible for religious experiencing are directly caused by God, as Swinburne comes near to suggesting,[28] then the nature of religious experiencing will be radically changed. Instead of being a free human response to a sense of the presence of the divine reality, we would have human brains being directly reprogrammed by a divine manipulator. But this would be false to the nature of the experience, whose ambiguity and diversity clearly indicate that it is a genuinely free response to a divine disclosure which we are epistemically free to accept or reject. The only other alternative is to posit some anthropological or psychological explanation for religious experiencing which robs it of evidential significance, imposes alien categories upon it and eliminates the claims of persons to relate in any significant sense to divine reality.

There is no need to follow this course. Most criticisms of dualism are addressed to views which are not held, or which need not be held, by a contemporary dualist. Of course, embodiment is central to most of our perceptions and any quasi-solipsistic account of mental life has to be false. There is no need for dualism to be in error on such matters, or to make the category mistakes so often attributed to it. In practice a thoroughgoing interactionist dualist and an exponent of brain–mind identity will be in complete agreement about how they see the world at least 99.9 per cent of the time, even though great importance attaches to those areas where they will differ. Within such areas religious experiencing will be much the most significant for human life, and within the field of religious experiencing what happens to people near death seems one of the most helpful fields of study.

The importance of near-death experiences (NDEs) is that they offer strong support for dualism, and also often contain religious elements which appear to be common across the cultures of the world. The most evidential features of the NDE are that persons report 'going out of the body' at the time of apparent death, they 'look down from above' on the resuscitation attempts, and they are incredibly accurate in the observations they subsequently report which turn out to be correct in terms of what a person would have seen if he or she really had been viewing from the ceiling. These facts are accepted even by the most resolutely sceptical of the NDE inquirers, Susan Blackmore. She accepts that 'there is no doubt that people describe reasonably accurately events that have occurred around them during their NDE'. However, she suggests that a combination of 'prior knowledge, fantasy, and lucky guesses and the remaining operating senses of hearing and touch' may provide the information for the images seen, which are viewed autoscopically from above because that is the perspective from which we see ourselves in memory.[29] People who actually have the experience always see such explanations as alien interpretations which fail to account for the way the experience actually seems to them. And the very large number of correct observations which do not fit into any of Blackmore's explanatory categories (other than the catch-all category of 'lucky guesses') suggests that the data cannot be accommodated in so narrow a Procrustean bed. As with other human experiences, it seems better to use Swinburne's 'Principle of Credulity': that, 'in the absence of special considerations', 'how things seem to be is good grounds for a belief about how things are'.[30] On that basis, 'out-of the-body' observations in the near-death state provide grounds for thinking that dualism may be true.

When consciousness of NDEs burst upon the world in 1973 with the publication of Moody's book *Life after Life*,[31] they appeared to be a wholly new phenomenon arising out of the ability of modern medicine to resuscitate people. Yet once NDEs came to be studied more closely it became apparent that they had much in common with elements in religious and mystical experiences reported throughout the ages in connection with religious figures in many human cultures. For example, Mircea Eliade suggests that in primal religions ideas about life after death may have originated in accounts of Shamanistic trances, which characteristically include a notion of the Shaman leaving his body.[32]

Most out-of-the-body experiences occur near the point of death. One therefore wonders whether it is the fact of such reported experiences that has given rise to the traditional description of death as the moment when the soul leaves the body. The experience of simply watching a person die leads to a much simpler picture of death as the moment when the person breathes-out (expires) for the last time. The fact that this description has been felt to need supplementation suggests that other facts of human experiencing have been given weight as well as what is most immediately apparent.

However, it is not simply in primal religions that there seem to be elements suggestive of foundational NDEs. They also appear to have played a key role in shaping belief in a future life in some of the major religious traditions. For example, in a Jewish mystical text called the *Zohar* we read: 'We have learned that at the hour of a man's departure from the world, his father and relatives gather round him and he sees and recognises them ... and they accompany his soul to the place where it is to abide.'[33] The question arises, how did they 'learn' this? One possible answer might be from reported NDEs. For modern NDE experiencers frequently report precisely such 'meetings' with deceased relatives, and hence an early NDE account may have been the source of this 'learning'. Likewise, in Zoroastrianism it is intriguing that the name of their deity, Ahura Mazda, literally means 'Being of Light'. This almost inevitably suggests that something akin to an NDE experience gave rise to this tradition. In Greek thought Plato played a key role in establishing the idea of the immortality of the soul, and in his book the *Republic* he says that the source of his belief was a story he had been told of a soldier from Er who was thought to have been killed in battle but who just before his cremation had 'come back to life and told the story of what he had seen in the other world'.[34]

Within Christianity the peak of mystical experience has always been described in terms of 'ecstasy', which literally means 'standing outside' the body. When St Paul found his religious authority challenged by the Corinthians he rested his claim to their respect explicitly on an experience which reads very much like a contemporary NDE:

> I know a Christian man who fourteen years ago (whether in the body or out of the body, do not know God knows) was caught up as far as the third heaven. And I know that this same man (whether in the body or apart from the body, I do not know-God knows) was caught up into paradise, and heard words so secret that human lips may not repeat them. About such a man I am ready to boast.[35]

St Paul was speaking autobiographically here, as a few verses later he laments that 'to keep me from being unduly elated by the magnificence of such revelations I was given a thorn in the flesh ... to keep me from being too elated'.[36] St Paul's experience included out-of-the-body experiences and visions of paradise, both of which are key features of the near-death experience.

Commenting on these verses, St John of the Cross, the great sixteenth-century mystic, remarked that such experiences normally only occur when the soul 'goes forth from the flesh and departs this mortal life'. But St Paul was allowed these visions by special grace. Such visions, however, occur 'very rarely and to very few for God works such things only in those who are very strong in the spirit and in the law of God'.[37] St John of the Cross had almost certainly had a comparable experience himself, as evidenced by his poems, where he speaks of 'living without inhabiting himself', as 'dying yet I do not die' and as 'soaring to the heavens'.[38]

In Islam it is clear that a strong ecstatic element was present in all Muhammad's revelatory experiences. He said: 'Never once did I have a revelation without feeling that my soul was being torn away from me.'[39] More significantly, his 'night journey', in which he ascended through the seven heavens, has been interpreted in the Sufi tradition as an 'annihilation' (fana) followed by 'revival' (baqa) in which Muhammad passed through death to the vision of God, and was then restored to life with a greatly enhanced spirituality.[40]

Professor Carl Becker claims that in Mahayana Buddhism the establishment in China of beliefs about being born in Buddha's Pure-Land 'clearly depend upon the remarkable death-bed and visionary experiences' of Chinese religious authorities from the fourth to the seventh centuries, just as the Japanese doctrines about Amida Buddha greeting the dying person are based on the visions and experiences of Japanese monks from the tenth to the twelfth centuries.[41] Likewise, Sogyal Rimpoche shows that in Tibetan Buddhism NDEs have long been acknowledged as religiously significant in that 'returnees from death' (deloks) have for centuries been regarded as important witnesses concerning the reality of the next (bardo) world.[42]

The contemporary importance of such traditions can be seen if one compares what Tibetan and Pure-land scriptures say with what contemporary experiencers report. For example, many near-death experiencers report looking down on their bodies and observing the distress of their relatives and the activities on the medical staff. So, too, in The Tibetan Book of the Dead we read that when the person's 'consciousness-principle gets outside its body' he sees his relatives and friends gathered round weeping and watches as they remove the clothes from the body or take away the bed.[43]

Seventy-two per cent of contemporary near-death experiencers report seeing a radiant light, which they often describe as a loving presence and sometimes name in accordance with a religious figure from their own tradition. A few experience a review of their past life, and many experience a range of mental images which have led many commentators to suggest that the next stage of existence could be a mind-dependent world. Once again this is precisely what the *Tibetan Book* says, for it speaks of the dying person seeing the radiant, pure and immutable light of Amida Buddha before passing into what is explicitly described as a world of mental images.

Concerning the Being of Light which contemporary experiencers see and name in accordance with their own tradition, this also is in accord with *The Tibetan Book of the Dead,* where we read, 'The *Dharmakaya* [deity] of clear light will appear in whatever shape will benefit all beings.' Commenting on this verse for his English translation, Lama Kazi Dawa-Samdup says:

> To appeal to a Shaivite devotee, the form of Shiva is assumed; to a Buddhist the form of the Buddha ... to a Christian, the form of Jesus; to a Muslim the form of the Prophet; and so for other religious devotees; and for all manner and conditions of mankind a form appropriate to the occasion.[44]

The place where contemporary experience and foundational beliefs come closest together is in Pure-land Buddhism. Many resuscitated people speak of seeing and being welcomed into the world beyond by a wonderful and gracious 'Being of Light'. They often claim that this being knows them completely and has limitless compassion to them in welcoming them into the life beyond. It is interesting that this is remarkably like what the Pure-land scriptures say: 'The Buddha of Infinite Light and Boundless Life' (*Amida*) has vowed to appear at the moment of death. Consequently, when people 'come to the end of life they will be met by Amida Buddha and the Bodhisatvas of Compassion and Wisdom and will be led by them into Buddha's Land'.[45] This combination of radiant light, wisdom and compassion corresponds precisely to the descriptions given by the resuscitated of their experience of this encounter.

What I suggest that if one looks back across the religious traditions of the world and the testimony of some key religious figures in both East and West, one sees constant parallels to what is currently being reported by many contemporary near-death experiencers. The big difference is in the relative number of such reports. We noted earlier that St Paul regarded his experience as giving him unique insight and authority; St John of the Cross speaks of the experience as coming very rarely and to very few; and Islam has always treated the experiences of Muhammad as something restricted to a very select group of prophets throughout human history who have had a distinctive call. The same is true in the Far East: NDEs used to happen to relatively few people, who often gained religious authority in consequence. What I suggest is that modern medical technology has, as it were, 'democratized' and made available to thousands an experience which has from the beginning lain at the heart of much of the world's religious perceiving and formed an important experiential basis for the future hope.

Another feature that NDEs have in common with other kinds of religious experiencing is that the NDE frequently leads to a change of lifestyle and to an enduring sense of the value and purpose of life. Long ago William James argued that religious experiences are real because they have real effects. In the case of the NDE this is particularly noticeable. Bruce Greyson, editor of Near-Death Studies and a professor of Psychiatry, sums up the data thus: 'It is the most profound experience I know of ... nothing affects people as strongly as this.'[46] This is further endorsed by Kenneth Ring, who shows that the most impressive feature of the NDE is the impact it has on the beliefs and attitudes of those who have them.[47] Of course, as with all such experiences, the impact is not epistemically coercive, so that it remains possible for a person to be unpersuaded by it. Nevertheless, for most people NDEs in particular and religious experiencing in general may reasonably be interpreted as providing evidential support for the validity of believing that human beings may at times encounter a reality which transcends the purely natural experiencing of our everyday life.

11

The contribution of Modernism to the contemporary understanding of world religion

The Modernist movement was at its height before Britain became a significantly pluralist society. Consequently, the relationship between Christianity and other faiths was not a burning issue during that period. Hence, although individual Modernists such as B. H. Streeter or A. C. Bouquet encouraged the study of 'comparative religion', many expositions of Modernist thought say very little about religions other than Christianity, and what they do say is often disparaging. John Lithgow points out that M. G. Glazebrook's work *The Faith of a Modern Churchman* says nothing about them; Henry Major's *English Modernism* has three brief references, in one of which they are described as 'inferior'; and R. D. Richardson's *Gospel of Modernism* thinks that 'all religions except Christianity and Buddhism can be instantly dismissed' by the grading scheme that he proposes.[1] Similarly, the only MCU conference devoted to world religion, before a series chaired by John Hick in the 1980s, was one held in 1922, and that went under the assertive title 'Christianity as the World Religion', with a paper from the future MCU president W. R. Matthews on 'The finality of Christianity'. It may therefore seem perverse to suggest that Modernism can make a significant contribution to the present debate when it failed to make an impact at the time of its greatest influence.

This would not be a fair judgement, however, because in evaluating any movement's position one has to see it in comparison with its contemporaries. At a time when most Christians adopted an 'exclusivist' attitude to other faiths, and sought to displace them, the Modernists adopted a 'fulfilment' model. In other words, they believed that God was at work in other religions preparing the ground for the future disclosure of Christ. Thus, according to

Henry Major, in the eyes of a Modernist other religions are 'preparatory to Christianity, and although inferior are not essentially alien. Christianity does not so much strive to replace them as to perfect them.'[2] I do not claim that attitudes such as these are helpful to our present situation. The most one can say is that the position of Modernists such as Major was far more positive than the totally negative approach to other faiths that was becoming increasingly popular at that time under the influence of Karl Barth's Neo-orthodoxy.

However, I believe that there are key features of Modernist theology which have an important contribution to make to contemporary Christian attitudes to, and beliefs about, other world faiths. The most important of these is the Modernist rediscovery of the importance of the Logos doctrine within early Christianity and its relevance to the present. For the earliest Christians the expression *Logos* was understood to refer to the concept of a universal presence of God working in all human beings. Hence to accept the Logos doctrine is necessarily to see all world religions as inspired by the same divine initiative. This was most clearly spelt out in the quotation from William Temple already cited in my Christology chapter:

> All that is noble in the non-Christian systems of thought, or conduct, or worship is the work of Christ upon them and within them. By the Word of God – that is to say by Christ – Isaiah, and Plato, and Zoroaster, and Buddha, and Confucius conceived and uttered such truths as they declared. There is only one divine light; and every man in his measure is enlightened by it.'[3]

Temple's use of the word 'Christ' is confusing and inappropriate in this setting and reflects his growing love for traditional language during his later life.[4] Despite this linguistic lapse, it nevertheless remains clear that the term *Logos* refers to the Stoic principle of a universal divine presence in human beings, and is not referring to the historical Jesus directly. Rather, it has reference to that working of God which, in Temple's view, inspired not only Jesus, but also Plato, Zoroaster, Buddha and Confucius, and by implication all other great religious thinkers as well. And to make this claim is to make a monumental shift in attitude from the exclusivist Christian position that had become normative over most of the Christian centuries. The revival of the Logos doctrine was thus of immense importance. Hick sees that the usage of Logos terminology is dynamic:

If, selecting from our Christian language, we call God-acting-towards-mankind the Logos, then we must say that *all* salvation within all religions is the work of the Logos and that under their various images and symbols men in different cultures and faiths may encounter the Logos and final salvation.[5]

In fact the Logos terminology as revived by the Modernists provides Hick with a foundation of thought which goes quite as far as the view which came to be expressed in his Gifford Lectures, *An Interpretation of Religion*: namely, that all religions are human responses to a single divine reality.[6]

Such a perspective is similarly helped by taking further than the Modernists originally did the full implications of their 'degree Christology'. In principle a degree Christology ought to prevent any absolutizing of the divine presence in Jesus Christ that treats as irrelevant the awareness of divine reality disclosed through the lives of others. By contrast, the traditional view that the way God was present in Christ was different in kind from God's presence elsewhere carries the implication that Christianity is different in kind from other faiths. Such an attitude leads to an arrogant sense that all truth about God is to be found within the Christian tradition and that any insights that other faiths may have are valid if and only if they agree with what Christianity teaches. Dialogue becomes pointless when one side believes it has all the answers. However, a full acceptance of all the implications of a degree Christology will recognize that the most that can be claimed in relation to Jesus is that his life and teaching give us great insight into the character and personality of God. However, the fact that he was mistaken about God's purposes in that he supposed that history would soon end, and that he took for granted the reality of evil spirits, shows that even his religious insights were limited to those available to a human being living at that time. Hence, a contemporary person, of whatever faith, who recognizes that history is likely to continue and that its course is not actually being affected by demonic agencies has in at least these particulars a truer insight into reality than that enjoyed by the historical Jesus. A Christian may still believe that in Jesus the divine appeared in as pure a form as it *has appeared* on earth (so far); but the absolute claim 'as pure a form as it can appear on earth'[7] will be recognized as going beyond the evidence. The relativizing of the divine claims made about Jesus in a degree Christology make possible a recognition that many other religious teachers, including the prophets of the Hebrew Bible and the saints and Doctors of the Church as well as Plato, Zoroaster, Confucius, Buddha and leaders of other great religious traditions including Muhammad, Guru Nanak and Shinran, were also channels of the divine spirit.

The second contribution the Modernists make to contemporary thought is their insistence that universal salvation is a free gift and is in no sense the product of Jesus' death on the cross. Hastings Rashdall's work *The Idea of the Atonement in Christian Theology*, published in 1919, was regarded by all Modernists as having definitively shown that the cross effected no change in God and that Jesus died neither as bait for the Devil nor to 'placate' the Father.[8] This means that when we approach other religions we should not seek to include them inside a Christian bracket which sees Jesus' death as the necessary means for salvation. According to Pope John Paul II, 'every human being without any exception whatever has been redeemed by Christ'.[9] This 'inclusivist' position is an enormous improvement on earlier Catholic teaching, such as that of the Council of Florence of 1438–45, which declared: 'No one remaining outside the Church, not just pagans, but also Jews or heretics or schismatics, can become partakers of eternal life; but they will go to the everlasting fire prepared for the devil and his angels unless before the end of life they are joined to the Church.'[10] Yet it still remains the case that to say that 'everyone has been redeemed by Christ' is to devalue other faiths as ways of salvation. It also presupposes an understanding of God which Hastings Rashdall showed to be open to very serious objection both on ethical grounds (in that it is morally offensive to suggest that the Father's wrath was propitiated by the death of the Son) and on doctrinal grounds (in that it implies a tritheistic understanding of the Trinity).[11]

A third contribution of the Modernists is their insistence on the importance of religious experiencing as one of the foundations of faith. Inevitably this also will lead in the direction of accepting the validity of other religions. For if persons of faith feel justified in believing as they do on the basis of what they believe they have experienced, they have to accept that others whose experiences were moulded within another religious tradition have an equal right to trust the validity of their own religious experiencing as justifying their own commitment. This has certainly been a powerful factor in encouraging openness to people of other faiths. For example, in the mid-nineteenth century Rowland Williams became convinced that genuine faith is based not on the authority of the Bible, but, rather, on the individual experience of the believer. He sought to demonstrate this by pointing out that in the Bible itself Enoch walked with God, Melchizedek blessed Abraham, and Abraham's faith was counted to him for righteousness centuries before the earliest of our sacred books took their present form.[12] Later, when he came to study Hinduism in depth, he became aware that, like Christianity, it was based on profoundly felt religious experience. Hence, Williams felt compelled to entitle his comparative study of Christianity and Hinduism *The Knowledge of the Supreme Lord in Christianity and in Hinduism*.[13] Through his study of other faiths he became conscious that an awareness of God, which is common to most human traditions, is far more basic to Christianity than its distinctive beliefs about Christ, and hence he concluded:

We cannot acknowledge a Providence in Jewry without owning that it may have comprehended sanctities elsewhere. But the moment we examine fairly the religions of India and of Arabia, or even those of primaeval Hellas and Latium, we find that they appealed to the better side of our nature, and their essential strength lay in the elements of good which they contained.[14]

The moment one prioritizes religious experience as foundational then one is irresistibly led to recognize the divine presence in other faiths.

The experiential base of all the different world religions can be demonstrated if one looks at the nature of the human response to the divine. In almost all cases it manifests itself in worship. However much religions may differ, one is never really in any doubt that religious buildings have more in common with each other than with other buildings. Christianity and Buddhism are very different, and yet when I stood in the temple of Amida Buddha in Tokyo I felt an overwhelming sense that I was in a familiar kind of place. If a person could visit earth from a planet of some distant star and stand at the back of a temple, a gurdwara, a synagogue, a mosque or a church, he or she would have little doubt in sensing that in an important sense the same kind of activity was going on, however much cultural differences led to differing modes of expression. The similarity can be further demonstrated by reading through the hymns, prayers and religious readings used in different traditions. Provided that one removed the specific names which occur, one would regularly be at a loss to know from which tradition the prayer or hymn came, for the overlap of expression is so striking.

This point was made very vividly in a fascinating comparative study, *The Buddha and the Christ,* by a leading Modernist, B. H. Streeter, who shows how closely parallel have been some of the developments within Buddhism and Christianity, and how these have found expression in similarities of worship. Thus, anticipating Hick by more than forty years, Streeter argued that 'Mahayana stands to primitive Buddhism in a relation not unlike that of the Gospel according to St John to that according to St Matthew. That is to say, the interest has shifted from the teaching of the Founder to reflection on the meaning for religion of his life and person.'[15] Streeter shows how in Mahayana Buddhism in general, and in the Pure-land tradition in particular, Buddhism ceased to be interested in the personality of its founder and came instead to focus on a metaphysical belief in the identity of his Buddhahood with the Absolute.[16] This expressed itself in forms of worship in the great Buddhist temples, which have a remarkable resemblance to the Choir Office and the Mass in the cathedrals of Europe, including similarity of altar, vestments, chanting, ascending incense and even the manual acts of the priests.[17] Streeter also showed the similarity between the prayers and hymns of devotion to Amida Buddha in the Pure-land sect and similar hymns addressed to Christ within Christianity, even to the extent of Japanese Buddhists being happy to plagiarize from Christian hymns and sing:

> Buddha loves me this I know,
> For the Sutras tell me so.[18]

As one of the greatest New Testament scholars of his age, Streeter was vividly aware that the understanding of Christ in classic Christianity had 'travelled a long way from the New Testament', just as the devotee of Amida 'has travelled a long way from primitive Buddhism'.[19] However, that a parallel development has happened in two world religions makes an interesting point about the way in which human intuitions and longings colour the way people respond to the awareness of that which lies behind the religious experience of humankind.

There is another way in which Modernism can help to make sense of the plurality of world religions, and that is that Modernism can suggest a way of coping with the differences as well as with the similarities between the world religions. The problem with any attempt to fashion a global interpretation of the phenomenon of religion has always been the need to reconcile the notion that each religion is some sense an authentic response to the same divine reality, while at the same time facing up to the immense diversity in the ways in which that reality is pictured. The objection constantly levelled against theories of religious pluralism is that they overemphasize the similarities and do not do justice to the fundamental incompatibilities between the different religions. For example, John Austin Baker writes scathingly about 'fashionable nonsense about all faiths really saying the same thing or all paths in the end leading to the top of the same mountain'. Baker believes such talk is

> insulting to all believers and devalues rational thought in general. The God of Hinduism is not the same as the God of Islam . . . only in a world where all hope of discovering truth has been abandoned do people comfort themselves with the illusion that there is no ultimate difference between Yes and No.[20]

Such an onslaught indicates that Baker has not begun to take on board what the problem is all about. He does not actually believe that 'the God of Hinduism and the God of Islam' are ontologically distinct deities, because he acknowledges that all the philosophical and scientific arguments that suggest the possibility of God do so on the assumption that we are living in a universe of 'regularity and order'.[21] Polytheism is incoherent in this context, and this is explicitly acknowledged in all religious traditions as soon as they reach any kind of maturity. Nor is it justifiable to say that one only kind of worship corresponds to reality and all the rest are simply worshipping human projections, for there are no adequate criteria to make such a distinction. The problem, therefore, is how one can accept the authenticity of human religious experiencing while recognizing at the same time the enormous diversity of understanding concerning that which is the object or ground of that worship.

This problem usually focuses on the contradictory 'truth claims' in different world religions. For example, it is urged that it cannot be true both that Jesus is the Son of God and that 'God has not taken to himself a Son'.[22] It cannot be true both that God is best understood as personal and that the ultimate reality behind all things is impersonal. It cannot simultaneously be true that after death we will be raised to a new and glorious life and that after death we will either merge with the Absolute or return to live another life in another body on this earth. The existence of mutually incompatible beliefs is used to justify belief that not more than one religion can be true and that the rest must therefore be false, at least in all respects where they differ from the teaching of the religion favoured by the person making this kind of judgement.

Modernism can make an important contribution to this debate in two ways. First, because it has shown that over the centuries enormous differences in religious belief and understanding of a quite fundamental kind have existed within Christianity but that nevertheless ecumenically minded Christians have continued to feel able to see themselves as members of a single faith-community stretching across the world and across history. If this is possible within a single faith, might it not also be possible for the religious experience of humanity as a whole? Second, the Modernists have shown that if one does not simply take doctrinal statements at face value but tries to explore what they really mean, one will very often find that differences in expression often reflect different facets of human experiencing and may not in reality be as contradictory as they first seem. For example, it is by no means clear that what Muslims wish to deny by saying that 'that God has not taken to himself a Son' is the same as what Christians wish to affirm when they describe Jesus as 'Son of God'. After all, the early Christians always repudiated the idea that Jesus was a divine/human hybrid with an earthly mother and a heavenly father in the way that Heracles was believed in Greek mythology to be the product of a sexual union between Zeus and a young girl. The fact that Muslims have never had any difficulty in affirming the Virgin Birth of Jesus reminds us that that doctrine in itself in no way contradicts the point I have just made.

From the very beginnings of Modernist thought during the time of the Victorian 'crisis of faith', the problem of religious diversity within Christianity has been recognized. In his book *Rational Godliness,* published in 1855, for example, Rowland Williams argued that immense harm had been done to the Christian cause by people who treated Christian beliefs as if they had simply 'dropped from heaven'. By contrast, if one looks at Christianity historically one can see that it has never been a static religion, but has always been a living faith which has constantly grown and developed as human knowledge advances. Consequently, in a succession of generations 'very great changes may be expected to prevail in the way of expressing Christian truth'.[23]

The Modernists spelt out in detail just how great these differences have been. As we saw in chapter 2, for hundreds of years Christians believed in an infallible Bible, a six-day creation, a historical fall, an objective act of propitiatory atonement, and a hell to be damned into or redeemed from. Yet, as a result of the Modernist critique, almost no contemporary Christian intellectuals would speak of their faith in such terms. Indeed, I find that contemporary students of theology often find it hard to believe that any Christians could *ever* have believed such things as that the vast majority of the human race was to be tortured day and night for ever with an accumulation of every possible punishment, and that 'in order that the happiness of the saints [in heaven] may be more delightful to them . . . they will be given a perfect view of the sufferings of the damned'.[24] Yet this can be shown to have been not merely the official orthodoxy but also a widely held belief for hundreds of years.

Moreover, when we actually look at what different schools of thought within Christianity believe about God's essential nature and God's relation to the world, we find differences at least as wide as any that exist between Christianity and other faiths. Consider, for instance, the difference between the timeless God of mainstream Christian philosophy and the everlasting God of Biblical Theology. For timeless God, past, present and future exist simultaneously in an eternal 'now'. Such a God knows everything, including the future, which is as real to him as the present. Timeless God cannot change, suffer, or be affected by anything, but exists in eternal self-sufficiency. God is incomprehensible to us, for all human understanding works within the categories of time. Hence, as Aquinas and the dominant tradition of Catholic theology insist, we can only speak of God analogically. None of our language describes God as God is. By contrast, the God of the Bible exists in time, knows the past and present but cannot know the future. Such a God can much more readily be thought of in personal terms and we can believe that we have a relationship with such a God that matters to him in so far as he is changed by it.

Within contemporary Christianity many thinkers have moved away from belief in the timeless God of classic Christian philosophy and see God as existing within the temporal process. The problem with this is that modern physics shows that space and time are interrelated, so that a God who exists in time must also exist in space and hence be a finite being within the universe as the process theologians maintain, rather than exist as the all-transcendent creator. I have no intention of discussing here the merits of these two contrasting concepts of God. My sole concern is to highlight that they are fundamentally different concepts, quite as different as anything separating Christianity from other world faiths. Indeed, the everlasting God of Biblical Theology seems closer to the God of Islam or Judaism than to the God of classic Christian philosophy, while a timeless God might seem to have more in common with the Dharmakaya of Mahayana Buddhism than to a God who exists within the temporal process.

Whether God is timeless or everlasting also affects the Christian understanding of heaven. For in an eternity where time is no more nothing further can ever happen. The classic prayer *Requiem Aeternam* really did imply a state of total rest. As Augustine says, 'We shall rest in the sabbath of eternal life . . . in the repose which comes when time ceases.'[25] By contrast, everlasting life offers limitless possibilities of new experience over endless time. There is literally all the difference there could be between 'being brought to everlasting life', as promised in the 1662 Book of Common Prayer and being kept 'in eternal life', which is the replacement offered by the *Alternative Service Book* of 1980. This contrast can be vividly demonstrated by the responses to the death of Princess Diana. Many of the floral tributes expressed the hope that Diana and Dodi are now walking together in paradise in a new life freed from the pressures they encountered on earth. By contrast, Cardinal Hume, in the tradition of a timeless heaven, affirms that Diana has entered a place where 'God locks us for ever into that endless *now* of God's ecstatic love'.[26]

A second example of a fundamental difference between

Christians today lies in the way they understand prayer and providence. Much popular evangelical Christianity has taken over a traditional picture of God as the all-powerful controller of everything that happens. Hence, what happens to an individual or to society is seen as due directly to the will of God as the all-powerful, all-seeing and all-directing, ruler of the universe, without whose immediate involvement not even a sparrow would fall to the ground. It is axiomatic in many evangelical Churches that God is active in the world in this way. The *Alpha* course commended by many mainstream Church leaders for use in the instruction of new members takes the power of petitionary prayer and the reality of the miraculous for granted,[27] and in regular services all over the country petitionary prayers are offered up in simple trust, with no sense that serious theological issues are thereby raised.

Other Christians, by contrast, believe that God has created an autonomous universe governed by the laws of nature in which he does not intervene in particular cases to alter the course of nature or history, but instead shows his loving concern through his presence with us in our joys and in our sorrows. Such a view is taught in a report of the Church of England Doctrine Commission of 1987 called *We Believe in God*.[28] This explicitly repudiates belief in particular providence and teaches instead a theology which sees God not as an all-powerful controller, but as one whose loving concern is shown by his participation with us. In some areas of life rejection of belief in particular providence is widespread. For example, since the rise of modern weather-forecasting it has seemed increasingly embarrassing to pray for rain. In connection with the death of Princess Diana, no one has suggested that her crash in the tunnel was directly caused by God, as would undoubtedly have been taught and believed two centuries earlier. However, in many Churches explicitly petitionary prayers are confidently offered up, particularly in services of healing, in a way which only makes sense if it is still believed by the one leading the prayers that God can be expected to act in response to them. This suggests that two utterly different and mutually incompatible understandings of God and of God's relation to the world are co-existing side by side within many Christian Churches and in the confused thinking of many ordinary Christians.

The third difference I shall mention is that disclosed in different contemporary Christian attitutudes to people of other faiths. As late as 1991 one-fifth of the Anglican clergy in England and Wales signed a petition against any dialogue with people of other faiths, affirming their conviction that 'salvation is offered only through Jesus Christ', who is 'the only saviour' and 'the only way to God'.[29] If one reflects on the difference between the Christian exclusivist and the Christian universalist, it is hard to imagine a wider gulf than in their respective understandings of God. Both may worship together in the same church, and yet they hold utterly different and mutually incompatible pictures of God in their minds. The exclusivist thinks in holy awe of a God of such implacable wrath that the vast majority of humanity must be tortured for ever in the flames of hell. The universalist thinks of God as a loving heavenly Father who is always ready to forgive his prodigal children and whose will is that all shall be saved. I cannot think of any differences in ways of thinking about God between world religions that are wider than these two incompatible images. To accept the actuality of human religious experience while recognizing the tension of mutually incompatible belief-systems requires the acceptance of a pluralist solution not only for inter-faith dialogue, but also to do justice to the experience of everyday worshipping within the Christian Church.

Such differences inside Christianity illustrate the difficulty of objecting to pluralism on the grounds of the importance of different 'truth claims'. For it cannot be true both that God is temporal and that he is timeless. It cannot be true both that God determines everything that happens within the world and that he has created an autonomous universe. It cannot be true both that Jesus is the only way to God and that God has nowhere left himself without witness. These differences are vast in terms of how Christianity is to be understood. Experientially it seems simply to be the case that equally committed Christians differ profoundly from one another in the way they understand their faith. Both the reality of faith and the reality of doctrinal diversity must be accepted. But if one is to say this, one seems forced in the direction of a pluralist solution. On this hypothesis, if faith is valid, it is because it is a response to a transcendent reality, and the different ways in which Christians interpret this reality have to be understood as reflecting different cultures and different philosophical/scientific ways of understanding the nature of reality.

This does not mean, however, that Christian theologians should acquiesce in Hick's suggestion that, because great diversity of viewpoint exists within and between religions and because there are no universally agreed criteria, we must abandon all attempts to evaluate their various teachings. Hick is undoubtedly right to point out that as a matter of history all existing religions are a mixture of good and bad, and I accept that no purpose is served in seeking to grade the great world religions as total systems.[30] As the head of a department in which all the great religions are taught, and in which we seek to ensure that wherever possible they are taught from within, I fully accept that it would be utterly odious to seek to make any kind of blanket comparisons of one with another. But this does not mean that when one explores individual aspects of a religion's teaching one cannot apply tests of logic, coherence and evidence to them, as has long happened in the philosophy of religion and in modern doctrinal study.

The advantage of studying religion from a Modernist position is that Modernism has shown beyond any possible dispute the immense range of mutually incompatible beliefs that have been taught as Christianity. Modernists have never hesitated to reject beliefs which Christians have held in the past but which conflict with what modern knowledge has shown us about the nature of reality. Hence, there is no question of claiming that all Christian beliefs are true and, by implication, that any conflicting beliefs in other traditions must be false. In every case one has the challenge of looking at a belief and asking oneself the grounds for supposing it to be true, from whichever religious tradition that belief has come. In my own study of beliefs about life after death, for example, I have found it immensely enriching to draw on what a variety of religious traditions have taught. The same is true in relation to exploring the problem of evil or the arguments for the existence of God. Just as philosophical study is enriched by drawing on a variety of traditions, so is the study of religion enriched by seeking to make use of as much of the religious experience and understanding of humanity as one can have access to.

Notes

Notes to Preface

1 Alan Stephenson, *The Rise and Decline of English Modernism* (London, SPCK 1984).
2 R. J. Page, *New Directions in Anglican Theology* (London, Mowbray, 1965), 138.

Notes to chapter 1: What is Modernism?

1 A. M. G. Stephenson cites thirteen books in favour of Modernism and four against, all of which included the noun or adjective prominently in their titles. Cf. his work *The Rise and Decline of English Modernism* (London, SPCK, 1984), 12–13. His list is by no means exhaustive: for example, it does not include C. J. Cadoux, *The Case for Evangelical Modernism* (London, Hodder, 1938).
2 Church of England Doctrine Commission, *Doctrine in the Church of England* (1938; reprinted SPCK, London, 1962).
3 H. D. A. Major's classic *English Modernism* (Cambridge, MA, Harvard University Press, 1927) is probably responsible for this terminology, despite the fact that he was a New Zealander and that his book was published in the USA. However, 'Anglican Modernism' would exclude writers such as Cadoux, and while 'English-speaking Modernism' would acknowledge the contribution of American, Welsh and Scottish authors, the fact that the MCU held all its conferences in England suggests that perhaps the traditional term is inescapable.
4 Catholic Modernism was condemned by Pius X in the decree *Lamentabili* and the encyclical *Pascendi*.
5 Major, *English Modernism*, 9–10.
6 Stephenson, *The Rise and Decline of English Modernism*, 7–9.
7 Cited from the last of W. R. Inge's Bampton Lectures on *Christian Mysticism* (1918) by A. M. G. Stephenson, *The Rise and Decline of*

English Modernism, 73. (The allusion to an 'impregnable rock' is to a work by W. E. Gladstone defending biblicism.)

[8] Stephenson, *The Rise and Decline of English Modernism ,*79.

[9] Cited from Hastings Rashdall, *Anglican Liberalism* (1908), 106 by Alan Stephenson, *The Rise and Decline of English Modernism,* 61.

[10] Major, *English Modernism,* 140.

[11] F. D. A. Schleiermacher, *The Christian Faith* (Edinburgh, T. & T. Clark, 1928), 52.

[12] James Livingston, *Modern Christian Thought* (New York, Macmillan, 1971), 101.

[13] Stephenson, *The Rise and Decline of English Modernism,* 171–5.

[14] Ibid., x.

[15] Paul van Buren, *The Secular Meaning of the Gospel* (London, SCM Press, 1963).

[16] Thomas Altizer and William Hamilton, *Radical Theology and the Death of God* (Harmondsworth, Penguin, 1966).

[17] Don Cupitt, *Taking Leave of God* (London, SCM, 1980).

[18] R. J. Hollingdale, 'Introduction' to Friedrich Nietzsche, *Thus Spoke Zarathustra* (Harmondsworth, Penguin, 1961), 10.

[19] F. Nietzsche, '"The Gay Science": Aphorism 125', in W. Kaufmann, (ed.), *The Portable Nietzsche* (New York, Viking, 1954), 96.

[20] Cupitt, *Taking Leave of God.*

[21] *Paul Johnson,* 'Peaceful co-existence', *Prospect,* 7 (April 1996), 34–8.

[22] Terry Miethe and Antony Flew, *Does God Exist? A Believer and an Atheist Debate* (New York, Harper, 1991), 65.

[23] Keith Ward, *The Turn of the Tide: Christian Belief in Britain Today* (London, BBC Publications, 1986), 45.

[24] Russell Stannard, *Science and the Renewal of Belief* (London, SCM, 1982), cover.

[25] Paul Davies, *God and the New Physics* (London, J. M. Dent, 1983), ix. Cf. also his *The Mind of God* (London, Simon & Schuster, 1992).

[26] Kai Nielsen, *Contemporary Critiques of Religion* (London, Macmillan, 1971), 19; 'Foreword' to K. Parsons, *God and the Burden of Proof* (New York, Prometheus, 1989), 7.

[27] Richard Purtill, 'The current state of arguments for the existence of God', *Review and Expositor,* 82 (1985), 521.

[28] Basil Mitchell, *The Justification of Religious Belief* (London, Macmillan, 1973); Richard Swinburne, *The Existence of God* (Oxford, Clarendon Press, 1991).

[29] Paul Badham, *A John Hick Reader* (London, Macmillan, 1990), 59.

[30] Open Letter Group, 'An invitation to the clergy of the Church of England', 20 Sept. 1991.

[31] M. Hammerton and A. C. Downing, 'Fringe beliefs among under-graduates', *Theology* 82, No. 690 (1979), 433–46.

[32] Allan Kellehear, *Experiences Near Death* (Oxford, Oxford University Press, 1996), 60 and 94.

[33] Tony Walter, 'Death and postmodern spirituality: a sociological response', a paper presented to the 21st International Conference on the Unity of Sciences, Washington DC, 24–30 Nov. 1997.

[34] Hastings Rashdall, *The Idea of Atonement in Christian Theology* (London, Macmillan, 1925).

Notes to chapter 2: Why Modernism was, and is, necessary

[1] Jude 1:3.

[2] Hebrews 13: 8.

[3] St Vincent of Lerins, 'Commonitorium', 2: 3, cited in F. L. Cross, *The Oxford Dictionary of the Christian Church* (London, Oxford University Press, 1958), 1423. Cf. Tom O' Loughlin, 'Newman, Vincent of Lerins and development', *Irish Theological Quarterly*, 58 (1991), 147–66.

[4] Edmund Burke, *Reflections on the Revolution in France,* cited in *The Oxford Dictionary of Quotations* (London, Oxford University Press, 1949), 102.

[5] Although this saying was attributed to Erasmus and appeared on the heading of *The Modern Churchman* for many years, no one can find it in any of Erasmus' own writing. It seems that H. D. A. Major invented it as epitomizing Erasmus' perspective.

[6] Rowland Williams, *Rational Godliness* (London, Bell & Daldry, 1855), ch. 24.

[7] Dennis Nineham, *Christianity, Medieval and Modern* (London, SCM, 1993), 234.

[8] J. W. Burgon, *Inspiration and Revelation,* 89; cited in J. E. Carpenter, *The Bible in the Nineteenth Century* (London, Longman, 1903), 7.

[9] J. W. Burgon, *Petra,* line 132, cited in *The Oxford Dictionary of Quotations* (London, Oxford University Press, 1949), 100.

[10] Cf. Article 9 of the *Thirty-Nine Articles of the Church of England* in the Book of Common Prayer, 1662.

[11] Cf. Revelation 14: 10–11.

[12] Tertullian, *De spectaculis,* ch. 30; cited in W. R. Alger, *The Destiny of the Soul* (1860; repr. New York, Greenwood Press, 1968), 513.

[13] Peter Lombard, *Sentences,* 4/50/7, cited along with many other horrific statements of this type in the work of the Modernist scholar Percy Dearmer, *The Legend of Hell* (London, Cassell, 1929), 34.

[14] St Thomas Aquinas, *Summa theologiae,* pt. III, supp. 94, art. 1; cited

in Dearmer, *The Legend of Hell*, 35.

15 J. S. Bezzant, 'Intellectual objections', in A. R. Vidler (ed.), *Objections to Christian Belief* (London, Constable, 1963), 85.

16 Cf. C. G. Gillispie, *Genesis and Geology* (New York, Harper, 1959).

17 F. S. Taylor, 'Geology changes the outlook', in H. Grisewood (ed.), *Ideas and Beliefs of the Victorians* (New York, Dutton, 1966), 192.

18 Carpenter, *The Bible in the 19th Century*, 171.

19 Rowland Williams, *Christianity and Hinduism* (Cambridge, Cambridge University Press, 1856), ch. 11.

20 Don Cupitt, *Crisis of Moral Authority* (London, Lutterworth, 1972), ch. 1.

21 Susan Budd, *Varieties of Unbelief* (London, Heinemann, 1977), ch. 5.

22 Alec Vidler, *The Church in an Age of Revolution* (Harmondsworth, Penguin, 1974), 112; drawing on Margaret Maison, *Search Your Soul, Eustace* (1961), 209.

23 Friedrich Schleiermacher, *On Religion* (1799; repr. New York, Harper Torchbooks , 1965).

24 Friedrich Schleiermacher, *The Christian Faith* (1830; repr. Edinburgh, T.& T. Clarke, 1960).

25 S. T. Coleridge, *Aids to Reflection* (1825; repr. London, Bohn, 1901), 103.

26 O. J. Brose, *F. D. Maurice* (Columbus, Ohio University Press, 1971), 202.

27 F. D. Maurice, *Theological Essays* (1853; 3rd edn., London, Macmillan, 1871), 14.

28 Ibid., 45.

29 John 1:9.

30 Maurice, *Theological Essays*, 48.

31 Ibid., 135.

32 2 Corinthians 5: 19.

33 Maurice, *Theological Essays*, 142.

34 Ibid., 144.

35 F. Higham, *F. D. Maurice* (London, SCM, 1947), 93.

36 Benjamin Jowett, *St Paul's Epistles* (London, John Murray, 1855), 468ff.

37 Rowland Williams, *Hebrew Prophets* (London, Williams and Norgate, 1866), pt.1, 222ff.

38 Aubrey Moore, 'The Christian doctrine of God', in C. Gore, *Lux Mundi* (London, John Murray, 1889), 99.

39 A. M. G. Stephenson, *The Rise and Decline of English Modernism* (London, SPCK, 1984), 242-9.

40 Church of England Doctrine Commission, *The Mystery of Salvation* (London, Church House Publishing, 1995), 199.

41 Vidler uses the expression 'Liberal Protestantism', but in Britain this was precisely the position of almost all Modernists: Alec Vidler, *Twentieth Century Defenders of the Faith* (London, SCM, 1965), 12.

42 *Sunday Times*, 7 Sept. 1997, and also the BBC CD of the funeral.

Notes to chapter 3: Modernism in relation to Neo-orthodoxy

1 F. R. Tennant, *Philosophical Theology* (Cambridge, Cambridge University Press, 1927, 1928).

2 S. Freud, *The Future of an Illusion* (London, Hogarth Press, 1962).

3 A. J. Ayer, *Language, Truth and Logic* (London, Gollancz, 1964).

4 Karl Barth, *The Knowledge of God and the Service of God* (London, Hodder, 1938).

5 Karl Barth, *Protestant Theology in the Nineteenth Century* (London, SCM Press, 1972).

6 H. Zahrnt, *The Question of God* (London, Collins, 1969), 66.

7 Karl Barth, 'The revelation of God as the abolition of religion', in Owen Thomas (ed.), *Attitudes toward Other Religions* (London, SCM, 1969), 101.

8 H. Zahrnt, *The Question of God*, 35.

9 Karl Barth, *Anselm: Fides Quaerens Intellectum* (London, SCM, 1960), 27.

10 Ibid., 22.

11 James Livingston, *Modern Christian Thought* (New York, Macmillan, 1971), 332.

12 Ibid., 329–30.

13 Karl Barth, *Church Dogmatics*, iv 1 247 and iv 2 354 in H. Gollwitzer, *Karl Barth, Church Dogmatics: A Selection* (Edinburgh, T. and T. Clarke, 1994), 119, 131.

14 John Bowden, *Karl Barth* (London, SCM, 1971), 16.

15 Richard Rubenstein and John Roth, *Approaches to Auschwitz* (London, SCM, 1987), 205.

16 Ibid., 208.

17 Gollwitzer, *Karl Barth, Church Dogmatics: A Selection*, 31.

18 Karl Barth, *A Shorter Commentary on Romans* (London, SCM, 1959), 132, 139.

19 Rubenstein and Roth, *Approaches to Auschwitz*, 205–8.

20 Barth, *A Shorter Commentary on Romans*, 144–7.

21 Gavin D'Costa, 'Christianity and other religions', in Dan Cohn-

Sherbok (ed.), *Many Mansions* (London, Bellew, 1992), 33.

22 Gollwitzer, *Karl Barth, Church Dogmatics: A Selection*, 221–3.

23 Ibid., 213.

24 Ibid., 194–229, especially 212, 222–3.

25 Eberhard Busch, *Karl Barth* (London, SCM, 1976), 185–6.

26 Bowden, *Karl Barth*, 77–85.

27 Karl Barth, *Dogmatics in Outline* (1949; London, SCM, 1962), 59.

28 Langdon Gilkey, *Religion and the Scientific Future* (London, SCM, 1970), 18ff.; cited in M. W. Worthing, *God, Creation and Contemporary Physics* (Minneapolis, Minn., Fortress Press, 1996), 31.

29 Henry Major, *English Modernism* (Cambridge, Mass., Harvard University Press, 1927), 103.

30 Wolfhart Pannenberg, 'Theological questions to scientists', in *The Sciences and Theology in the Twentieth Century*, ed. A. R. Peacocke (Notre Dame, Ind., University of Notre Dame Press, 1982), 3; cited in Worthing, *God, Creation and Contemporary Physics*, 32.

31 Barth, *Church Dogmatics*, ii/1/318; cited in Keith Ward, *Religion and Creation* (Oxford, Clarendon Press, 1996), 43.

32 Gollwitzer, *Karl Barth, Church Dogmatics: A Selection*, 148 (citing i/1/448).

33 Zahrnt, *The Question of God*, 21.

34 Livingston, *Modern Christian Thought*, 329–30.

35 Barth, *Church Dogmatics*, iv/2/171–80 (Gollwitzer, 96–110).

36 Ibid., iv/1/247 (Gollwitzer, 119).

37 John Goldingay (ed.), *Atonement Today* (London, SPCK, 1995).

38 Hastings Rashdall, *The Idea of Atonement in Christian Theology* (London, Macmillan, 1925), 305, 333, 375, 411.

39 Livingston, *Modern Christian Thought*, 399.

40 Karl Barth, *The Faith of the Church* (London, Fontana, 1950), 136–46.

41 Barth, *Dogmatics in Outline*, 155.

42 Collen McDannell and Bernhard Lang, *Heaven: A History* (New York, Vintage, 1990), 346.

43 Dietrich Bonhoeffer, *Letters and Papers from Prison* (London, SCM, 1967), 157.

44 Ibid., 153.

45 Karl Barth, *Evangelical Theology* (London, Fontana, 1965), 101.

46 Thomas Altizer and William Hamilton, *Radical Theology and the Death of God* (Harmondsworth, Penguin, 1966), 16.

47 Paul van Buren, *The Secular Meaning of the Gospel* (London, SCM, 1963), 98.

Notes to chapter 4: Modernism in relation to radical and non-realist theologies

1 Rudolf Bultmann, 'New Testament and mythology', in H. W. Bartsch (ed.), *Kerygma and Myth* (New York, Harper, 1961), 3.

2 Ibid., 39.

3 Ibid., 37.

4 Ibid., 40–1.

5 Dietrich Bonhoeffer, *Letters and Papers from Prison* (London, SCM, 1953), 56.

6 Ibid., 91.

7 Grace Davie, *Religion in Britain since 1945* (Oxford, Blackwell, 1994), 43.

8 Christoph Turke, *What Price Religion?* (London, SCM, 1997), viii and back cover.

9 Vladislav Arzenukhin, 'The present state of religion in post-Communist Russia', in Paul Badham and Vladislav Arzenukhin (eds.), *Religion and Change in Eastern Europe* (forthcoming).

10 *Times*, 23 Dec. 1997, 10.

11 Xinzhong Yao, 'Success or failure? Christianity in China', *History Today* (Sept. 1994), 8.

12 Gilles Keppel, *The Revenge of God* (Cambridge, Polity Press, 1994).

13 John Polkinghorne, *Scientists as Theologians* (London, SPCK, 1996), 3.

14 Graham Ward, *The Postmodern God* (Oxford, Blackwell, 1997), xl–xlii.

15 Hebrews 11: 6.

16 W. Montgomery Watt, *Muhammad* (Oxford, Oxford University Press, 1961), 21–2.

17 R. W. Church, *St Anselm* (London, Macmillan, 1899), 85.

18 St Anselm, *Prayers and Meditations* (Harmondsworth, Penguin, 1973), 265.

19 Ibid., 245.

20 Deuteronomy 6: 4, Mark 12: 30.

21 Psalm 119: 41–8, 1 John 5: 3.

22 Don Cupitt, *Life Lines* (London, SCM, 1986), 49.

23 Ibid., 55–6.

24 Ibid., 109–10.

25 John Burnaby, *Amor Dei* (London, Hodder, 1938).

26 Friedrich Schleiermacher, *On Religion* (1799; repr. New York, Harper, 1958), 15–36.

27 Don Cupitt, *Taking Leave of God* (London, SCM, 1980), 69.

28 Immanuel Kant, *Religion within the Limits of Reason Alone* (New

York, Harper, 1960), 171, 181, xxix.

[29] Cupitt, *Taking Leave of God*, 134–5.

[30] Roy McKay, *John Leonard Wilson, Confessor for the Faith* (London, Hodder, 1973).

[31] Cupitt, *Taking Leave of God*, 10.

[32] Ibid., 138.

[33] Ibid., 161.

[34] Burnaby, *Amor Dei*, 257.

[35] Austin Farrer, *Saving Belief* (London, Hodder, 1964), 140.

[36] Vladimir Lossky, *The Mystical Theology of the Eastern Church* (London, James Clarke, 1957), ch. 2.

[37] Cupitt, *Taking Leave of God*, 139.

[38] Rowan Williams, *The Wound of Knowledge* (London, Darton, Longman & Todd, 1979), 175.

Notes to chapter 5: Modern science and the arguments for God's existence

[1] Alan Stephenson, *The Rise and Decline of English Modernism* (London, SPCK, 1984), 212, 233.

[2] I. T. Ramsey (ed.), *Prospect for Metaphysics* (1961), 80; cited in Howard Root, 'Beginning all over again', in A. Vidler (ed.), *Soundings* (Cambridge, Cambridge University Press, 1964), 3.

[3] William Craig, citing J. R. Gott III, James E. Gunn, David Shramm and Beatrice M. Tinsley, 'Will the universe expand forever?', *Scientific American* (Mar. 1976), 65, in W. L. Craig and Q. Smith, *Theism, Atheism and Big Bang Cosmology* (Oxford, Clarendon Press, 1995), 43.

[4] Craig and Smith, *Theism, Atheism and Big Bang Cosmology*, 43.

[5] Cf. I. B. Zel'dovich and I. D. Novikov, 'Contemporary trends in cosmology', *Soviet Studies in Philosophy*, 14 (1976), 46–7; cited in Craig and Smith, *Theism, Atheism and Big Bang Cosmology*, 44.

[6] Antony Flew, 'Stephen Hawking and the mind of God', *Cogito* (Spring 1996), 59.

[7] Said on video, *Whose World? An Exploration of Science and Belief* by Adam Ford (London, CTVC, 1987). Cf. P. W. Atkins, *Creation Revisited* (Oxford, Freeman, 1992).

[8] Stephen Hawking, *Black Holes and Baby Universes* (London, Bantam, 1993), 159.

[9] William Lane Craig, *The Kalam Cosmological Argument* (London, Macmillan, 1979), 63.

[10] I. Kant, *Critique of Pure Reason* (1781) in Kemp Smith's translation (London, Macmillan 1964), 507–18.

[11] Richard Swinburne, *The Existence of God* (Oxford, Clarendon Press, 1979), 131–2.

[12] Craig and Smith, *Theism, Atheism and Big Bang Cosmology*, 57.

[13] *The Letters of David Hume*, ed. J. Y. T. Greig (Oxford, Clarendon Press, 1932), I, 187; cited in Craig and Smith.

[14] Craig and Smith, *Theism, Atheism and Big Bang Cosmology*, 61.

[15] Flew, 'Stephen Hawking and the mind of God', 57.

[16] Ninian Smart, *Philosophers and Religious Truth* (London, SCM, 1964), 104.

[17] Psalm 90: 2.

[18] My account is compressed from Keith Ward, *Religion and Creation* (Clarendon Press, Oxford, 1996), 295.

[19] Ibid., 295; summarizing ch. 8 of Stephen Hawking, *A Brief History of Time* (London, Bantam, 1988).

[20] Hawking, *A Brief History of Time*, 141.

[21] Oliver Leamann, *Medieval Islamic Philosophy* (Cambridge, Cambridge University Press), 1985, ch. 1.

[22] Keith Ward, *God, Chance and Necessity* (Oxford, One World, 1996), 25.

[23] Ward, *Religion and Creation*, 296.

[24] Ibid., 295.

[25] John Hick, *An Interpretation of Religion* (London, Macmillan 1989) 82.

[26] Cafer Yaran, 'Scientific objectivity and theistic belief', an unpublished paper based on his Ph.D. thesis 'The Argument from Design in Contemporary Thought' (University of Wales, Lampeter, 1994).

[27] Hawking, *A Brief History of Time*, 127.

[28] John Leslie, *Universes* (London, Routledge, 1989), 29, 37, 3, 28.

[29] Brandon Carter, 'Large number coincidences and the anthropic principle in cosmology' (1974); repr. in John Leslie (ed.), *Philosophical Cosmology and Philosophy* (New York, Macmillan, 1990), 27; in Cafer Sadyk Yaran, 'Scientific objectivity and scientific belief', *In Depth* (Winter 1996), 84.

[30] John D. Barrow and Frank J. Tipler, *The Anthropic Cosmological Principle* (Oxford and New York, Oxford University Press, 1986), 22.

[31] Carter, 'Large number coincidences', 27.

[32] Paul Davies, *The Mind of God: Science and the Search for Ultimate Meaning* (London, Simon & Schuster, 1992), 213.

[33] Ibid., 21.

[34] Leslie, *Universes*, 6–8.

[35] William Lane Craig, 'The teleological argument and the anthropic principle' in W. L. Craig and M. S. Mcleod (eds.), *The Logic of Rational Theism: Explanatory Essays* (New York, Mellen, 1990), 142–3.

[36] Cited in John Leslie, 'Modern cosmology', in E. McMullin (ed.), *Evolution and Creation* (Notre Dame, Ind., Notre Dame University Press, 1985), 112.

[37] John Polkinghorne, 'A revived natural theology', in J. Fennema and I. Paul (eds.), *Science and Religion: One World Changing Perspectives on Reality* (Utrecht, Kluwer, 1990), 88.

[38] Roger Penrose, *The Emperor's New Mind* (London, Oxford University Press, 1989), 444–5.

[39] Interview recorded in a video (see note 7 above).

[40] Cited in Davies, *The Mind of God*, 223.

[41] Cited in Timothy Ferris, *The Whole Shebang* (London, Weidenfeld & Nicolson, 1997), 305.

[42] Paul Davies, *God and the New Physics* (London, Dent, 1983), ix.

[43] Ward, *God, Chance and Necessity*, 38.

[44] Ward, *Religion and Creation*, 296.

[45] Keith Ward, *God, Chance and Necessity*, 22.

[46] Leslie, *Universes*, 2.

[47] Ibid., 22.

[48] Ibid., 2.

[49] Ibid., 167.

[50] W. R. Inge, *The Philosophy of Plotinus* (London, Longman, 1929), xi.

[51] John Leslie, *Universes*, 2.

[52] Ward, *God, Chance and Necessity*, 28.

[53] Ward, *Religion and Creation*, 296.

[54] Inge, *The Philosophy of Plotinus*, (II), xii.

[55] Church of England Doctrine Commission, *Doctrine in the Church of England* (London, SPCK, 1992), 51.

[56] A. R. Peacocke, *Theology for a Scientific Age* (Oxford, Blackwell, 1990), 183.

[57] John Polkinghorne, *Science and Creation* (Boston, Mass., Shambala, 1989), 35.

[58] John Polkinghorne, *Serious Talk* (London, SCM, 1995), 77.

Notes to chapter 6: Modern confidence in the historical Jesus

[1] Amida Buddha's vows in *Sukhavativyuha-sutra*, vol. 1 (The Pureland sutra) *Bukkyo Dendo Kyokai, The Teaching of Buddha* (Tokyo, Buddhist Promoting Foundation, 1980), 202.

[2] *The Tome of Leo to Flavian*, T. B. Bindley, *Oecumenical Documents of the Faith* (London, Methuen, 1950), 227.

[3] Eusebius, *The History of the Church* (Harmondsworth, Penguin, 1965), 254.

[4] Adolf Harnack, *What is Christianity?* (1901; repr. London, Benn, 1958), 31.

[5] Ibid., 120.

[6] Ibid., 96.

[7] Ibid., 108–10.

[8] A. M . Ramsey, *From Gore to Temple* (London, Longman, 1960), 62.

[9] E.g. N. Smith, 'The centrality of Jesus'; J. W. Hunkin, 'Jesus as the revealer of God'; R. H. Lightfoot, 'What do we know of Jesus', all in *Modern Churchman*, 11 (Sept. 1921).

[10] Alister McGrath, *Christian Theology: An Introduction* (Oxford, Blackwell, 1994), 323.

[11] Rudolf Bultmann, *Jesus and the Word* (London, Fontana, 1958), 14.

[12] Geza Vermes, *The Religion of Jesus the Jew* (London, SCM, 1993), 2.

[13] R. H. Lightfoot, *History and Interpretation in the Gospels* (London, Hodder, 1935), 225.

[14] E. P. Sanders, *The Historical Figure of Jesus* (Harmondsworth, Penguin, 1993), xiii.

[15] G. Bornkamm, *Jesus of Nazareth* (London, Hodder, 1960).

[16] Sanders, *The Historical Figure of Jesus*, xiii, 10.

[17] J. P. Meier, *A Marginal Jew* (London, Chapman, 1993); James Dunn, *The Evidence for Jesus* (London, SCM 1985); N. T. Wright, *The New Testament and the People of God* (London, SPCK, 1992); J. L. Houlden, *Jesus: A Question of Identity* (London, SPCK, 1992).

[18] Martin Goodman, *The Ruling Class of Judaea* (1987); cited in Vermes, *The Religion of Jesus the Jew*, 3.

[19] Richard A. Burridge, *What are the Gospels? A Comparison with Graeco-Roman Biography* (Cambridge, Cambridge University Press, 1992).

[20] Sanders, *The Historical Figure of Jesus*, 3–4.

[21] A. E. Harvey, *Jesus and the Constraints of History* (1982), 6; cited in Vermes, *The Religion of Jesus the Jew*, 3.

[22] Graham Stanton, *The Gospels and Jesus* (Oxford, Oxford University Press, 1989), 272.

[23] Vermes, *The Religion of Jesus the Jew*, 215.

[24] Stanton, *The Gospels and Jesus*, 274.

[25] Vermes, *The Religion of Jesus the Jew*, 210.

[26] Ibid., 4.

[27] Adrian Thatcher, *Truly a Person, Truly God* (London, SPCK, 1990), 77.

[28] James Dunn, *Christology in the Making* (London, SCM, 1980), 60.

[29] E. Kasemann, *Essays on New Testament Themes* (London, SCM, 1964); E. Fuchs, *Studies of the Historical Jesus* (London, SCM, 1964); J. Robinson, *The New Quest of the Historical Jesus* (London, SCM 1966).

[30] Gunther Bornkamm, *Jesus of Nazareth* (London, Hodder, 1966), 53.

[31] Houlden, *Jesus: A Question of Identity*, 53.

[32] G. B. Caird, *Saint Luke* (Harmondsworth, Penguin, 1963), 48.

[33] Vermes, *The Religion of Jesus the Jew*, 4.

[34] C. F. D. Moule, *The Significance of the Message of the Resurrection for Faith in Jesus Christ* (London, SCM, 1968), 114–18.

[35] H. W. Bartsch, *Kerygma and Myth* (New York, Harper, 1961), 38.

[36] Sanders, *The Historical Figure of Jesus*, 280.

[37] McGrath, *Christian Theology*, 326.

[38] A. M. Ramsey, *From Gore to Temple* (London, Longman, 1960), 70.

[39] This is how Hans Kung differentiated his own position from that of earlier liberals: see H. Haring and Karl-Josef Kuschel, *Hans Kung: His Work and His Way* (London, Fount, 1979), 161.

[40] Hans Kung, *On Being a Christian* (London, Collins, 1977), 126–65, 214ff.

[41] Ibid., 444.

Notes to chapter 7: Modern ways of understanding the divinity of Christ

[1] Geza Vermes, *The Religion of Jesus the Jew* (London, SCM, 1993), 215.

[2] Hans Kung, *On Being a Christian* (London, Collins, 1977), 154.

[3] The tenth anathema of the Second Council of Constantinople, in J. Neuner and J. Dupuis, *The Christian Faith* (London, Collins, 1983), 162.

[4] I derive these definitions from the relevant entries in F. L. Cross (ed.), *The Oxford Dictionary of the Christian Church* (Oxford, Oxford University Press, 1958).

[5] E. L. Mascall, *Whatever Happened to the Human Mind* (London, SPCK, 1980), 84, citing St Gregory Nazianzus: see V. Lossky, *The Mystical Theology of the Eastern Church* (London, J. Clarke, 1957), 153.

[6] Ibid., 84.

[7] St Thomas Aquinas, *Compendium theologiae*, II, 6.

[8] St Thomas Aquinas, *Summa theologiae*, III, 35, 8, and III, 40, 1; citing John 18: 37.

[9] 1 Corinthians 1: 24.

[10]   Hebrews 2: 17.

[11]   Sherman Johnson, *A Commentary on the Gospel According to St Mark* (London, Black, 1960), 204 (discussing Mark 12: 36).

[12]   Matthew 5: 13.

[13]   Mark 9: 18, 9: 1.

[14]   John Austin Baker, *The Foolishness of God* (London, DLT, 1970), 137–42, 312, 144.

[15]   Brian Hebblethwaite, 'Jesus, God incarnate', in M. Green (ed.), *The Truth of God Incarnate* (London, Hodder, 1977), 102.

[16]   Brian Hebblethwaite, *The Incarnation* (Cambridge, Cambridge University Press, 1987), 1–2.

[17]   Hastings Rashdall, *God and Man*, 95; cited in A. M. Ramsey, *From Gore to Temple* (London, Longman, 1960), 40.

[18]   Irenaeus, *Against Heresies*, II/33/1 (Edinburgh, T. & T. Clarke, 1867), I, 409–10.

[19]   Cited in John Hick (ed.), *The Myth of God Incarnate* (London, SCM, 1971), 171.

[20]   Adolf von Harnack, *What is Christianity?* (London, Benn, 1958), 110.

[21]   The *Authorized Version* favours the first and the *New English Bible* the second. *The Revised English Bible* and *The Jerusalem Bible* give both, and all commentaries agree that either meaning is possible and hence both shades of meaning are really present.

[22]   St Athanasius, *On the Incarnation*, ch. 17 (London, Mowbray, 1963), 45.

[23]   John 1: 9.

[24]   William Temple, *Readings in St John's Gospel* (London, Macmillan, 1963), 9.

[25]   Luke 5: 8, 7: 6.

[26]   Rudolf Otto, *The Idea of the Holy* (1917; repr. Harmondsworth, Penguin, 1959), 176.

[27]   Hastings Rashdall, 'Christ as Logos and Son of God', *Modern Churchman*, 11 (1921).

[28]   Hastings Rashdall, *Philosophy of Religion*, (1910; repr. Westport, Conn.: Greenwood Press, 1970), 180–1.

[29]   Cf. Ramsey, *From Gore to Temple*, 71–3.

[30]   J. Hick, '[Letter to the editors]', *Theology* 30 (1977), 205.

[31]   Frances Young, 'A cloud of witnesses', in Hick (ed.), *The Myth of God Incarnate*, 35.

[32]   F. D. E. Schleiermacher, *The Christian Faith* (1830; repr. Edinburgh, T. & T. Clarke, 1960), 387.

[33]   Irenaeus, *Against Heresies*, 4/20/7.

[34]   D. M. Baillie, *God Was in Christ* (London, Faber, 1961), 114–17.

[35] Harnack, *What is Christianity?*, 109–110.

[36] J. F. Bethune-Baker, 'Jesus as both human and divine', *Modern Churchman*, 9 (1921), 301.

[37] Kung, *On Being a Christian*, 449–50.

[38] John Hick, *The Metaphor of God Incarnate* (London, SCM, 1993), 105.

[39] E. P. Sanders, *The Historical Figure of Jesus* (Harmondsworth, Penguin, 1993), 238.

[40] Geza Vermes, *The Religion of Jesus the Jew* (London, SCM, 1993), 215.

[41] Hick, *The Metaphor of God Incarnate*, 110.

[42] John Lithgow, a former student of mine, wrote up the contrast between the 1921 and 1967 MCU Conferences for an MA 'Modernists and Radicals' (University of Wales, Lampeter, 1983).

Notes to chapter 8: The Modernist understanding of the resurrection of Jesus Christ

[1] Hastings Rashdall, *Doctrine and Development* (London, Methuen, 1898), 180.

[2] Kirsopp Lake, *The Historical Evidence for the Resurrection of Jesus Christ* (London, Williams & Norgate, 1907), 31.

[3] Peter Carnley, *The Structure of Resurrection Belief* (Oxford, Clarendon Press, 1987), 197.

[4] B. H. Streeter (ed.), *Foundations* (London, Macmillan, 1912), 134.

[5] John Lithgow, *Modernists and Radicals* (MA thesis, University of Wales Lampeter, 1983), 227.

[6] Ibid.

[7] Church of England Doctrine Commission, *Doctrine in the Church of England* (London, SPCK, 1960), 83–8.

[8] Ibid., 89.

[9] A. M. Ramsey, *The Resurrection of Jesus Christ* (London, Fontana, 1963), 72; C. F. D. Moule, *The Significance of the Message of the Resurrection for Faith in Jesus Christ* (London, SCM, 1968).

[10] Paul Badham, 'The relative validity of alternative Christian beliefs about life after death' (Ph.D. thesis, University of Birmingham, 1973).

[11] G. W. H. Lampe and D. M. Mackinnon, *The Resurrection* (London, Mowbray, 1966); Paul Badham, *Christian Beliefs about Life after Death* (London, Macmillan, 1973).

[12] Paul Avis, *The Resurrection of Jesus Christ* (London, DLT, 1993); S. Barton and G. Stanton, *Resurrection* (London, SPCK, 1994); Gavin D'Costa, *Resurrection Reconsidered* (London, One World, 1996); S.

Davies, D. Kendall and G. O'Collins, *The Resurrection* (Oxford, Oxford University Press, 1997).

[13] Peter Carnley, *The Structure of Resurrection Belief* (Oxford, Clarendon Press, 1987).

[14] Davis, Kendall and O'Collins, *The Resurrection*, 133.

[15] David Moller, 'Bishop Carey comes to Canterbury', *Reader's Digest* 138: 827 (Mar. 1991), 39.

[16] Matthew 28: 6; Mark 16: 6; Luke 24: 3; John 20: 7.

[17] John 20: 17, 20: 27.

[18] Collated from Rufinus, Apostles' Creed, para. 42; Revelation 20: 13; Augustine, *City of God*, 22/20; Rufinus, para. 43.

[19] Acts 1: 9–11. (Many ancient texts of the New Testament insert a comparably explicit statement into Luke 24: 51, and such a view also appears in the longer ending of Mark's Gospel, i.e. Mark 16: 9–19, which is absent from the earliest Greek Texts.)

[20] Acts 1: 9.

[21] As an example of the way the three-decker universe was described, see Augustine, *City of God*, 22/11. For fuller discussion and references, see Badham, *Christian Beliefs about Life after Death*, 58–63.

[22] Moule, *The Significance of the Message of the Resurrection for Faith in Jesus Christ*, 10.

[23] Luke 24: 31, 24: 36; John 20: 19, 20: 26.

[24] House of Bishops, *The Nature of Christian Belief* (London: Church House Publishing, 1986), 22.

[25] Don Cupitt, *Christ and the Hiddenness of God* (Cambridge, Lutterworth, 1971), 144.

[26] House of Bishops, *The Nature of Christian Belief*, 24–5.

[27] Carnley, *The Structure of Resurrection Belief*, 227.

[28] 1 Corinthians 15: 44.

[29] Luke 24: 39.

[30] Acts 2: 27; citing Psalm 16: 10.

[31] Mark 16: 8.

[32] Henry Major, *English Modernism* (Cambridge, Mass., Harvard University Press, 1927), 67.

[33] G. N. M. Tyrell, *Apparitions* (London, Duckworth, 1953), 77, 79, 54.

[34] John 20: 19; Luke 24: 31, 24: 51; Matthew 28: 17; John 20: 17.

[35] Michael Perry, *The Easter Enigma* (London, Faber, 1969) 141 (with altered tenses).

[36] Tyrell, *Apparitions*, 35.

[37] Douglas Davies, 'Contemporary belief in life after death', in Peter Jupp and Tony Rogers (eds.), *Interpreting Death* (London, Cassell, 1997), 139–40.

[38] K. Osis and E. Haraldsson, *At the Hour of Death* (New York, Avon, 1977), pp. 13–14.

[39] John Hick, *The Metaphor of God Incarnate* (London, SCM, 1993), 38.

[40] P. and L. Badham, *Immortality or Extinction?* (London, Macmillan, 1982), 93–5.

[41] Wolfhart Pannenberg, *Jesus, God and Man* (London, SCM, 1968), 108.

[42] James Dunn, *The Evidence for Jesus* (London, SCM, 1985), 61–2.

[43] I Corinthians 15: 13–17.

[44] 1 Peter 3: 18, 1: 3, 4: 6.

[45] Paul Badham, *Christian Beliefs about Life after Death*, part two.

[46] Church of England Doctrine Commission, *Doctrine in the Church of England*, 209; The Bishops of the Netherlands, *A New Catechism* (London, Burns & Oates, 1967), 479, 474, 473.

Notes to chapter 9: Modernist and contemporary views of life after death

[1] Paul Edwards, *Immortality* (New York, Macmillan, 1992), 329.

[2] W. R. Inge, *The Philosophy of Plotinus* (London, Longman, 1929).

[3] Church of England Doctrine Commission, *Doctrine in the Church of England* (1938; repr. London, SPCK, 1962), 207.

[4] Oscar Cullman, 'Immortality of the soul or resurrection of the dead', in K. Stendahl (ed.), *Immortality and Resurrection* (New York, Macmillan, 1965), 10. Note that Cullman had been making statements of this kind in many earlier publications going back at least to 1943.

[5] 1 Timothy 4: 16.

[6] James Barr, *Old and New in Interpretation* (London, SCM, 1966), 52.

[7] 1 Corinthians 15: 50.

[8] Eric C. Rust, *Nature and Man in Biblical Thought* (London, Lutterworth, 1953), 104.

[9] Ibid. Walter Eichrodt, *Theology of the Old Testament*, vol. 2 (London, SCM, 1967); and A. R. Johnson, *The Vitality of the Individual in the Thought of Ancient Israel* (Cardiff, University of Wales Press, 1964).

[10] 2 Maccabees 7.

[11] Robert Morgan, 'Flesh is precious', in S. Barton and Graham Stanton (eds.), *Resurrection* (London, SPCK, 1994), 16.

[12] For full discussion of this, see Paul Badham, *Christian Beliefs about Life after Death* (London, Macmillan, 1976; London, SPCK, 1978), ch. 3.

13 1 Corinthians 2: 9.

14 Church of England Doctrine Commission, *The Mystery of Salvation* (London, Church House Publishing, 1996), 10–11.

15 Ibid., 191–2.

16 Antony Kenny, *The God of the Philosophers* (Oxford, Clarendon Press, 1979).

17 Peter Jupp and Tony Rogers, *Interpreting Death* (London, Cassell, 1997), ch. 11.

18 Cited in John Hick, *Death and Eternal Life* (London, Macmillan, 1976), 218–19.

19 Ibid., 281ff.

20 J. Neuner and J. Dupuis, *The Christian Faith in the Doctrinal Documents of the Catholic Church* (London, Collins, 1983), 691.

21 *Catechism of the Catholic Church* (London, Chapman, 1994), 83, 227.

22 Richard Swinburne, *Is there a God?* (Oxford, Oxford University Press, 1996), 77.

23 Richard Swinburne, *The Evolution of the Soul* (Oxford, Clarendon Press, 1986), 1–2.

24 Keith Ward, *The Battle for the Soul* (London, Hodder, 1985), 149–50.

25 Paul and Linda Badham, *Immortality or Extinction?* (London, SPCK, 1984), 74.

26 Jacques Monod, *Chance and Necessity* (London, Collins, 1971), 30.

27 Paul Badham, 'God, the soul and the future life', in S. Davis (ed.), *Death and Afterlife* (London, Macmillan, 1989).

28 Hans Eysenck, *Sense and Nonsense in Psychology* (Harmondsworth, Penguin, 1957), 133.

29 Keith Campbell, *Body and Mind* (London, Macmillan, 1970), 91.

Notes to chapter 10: Modern religious experiencing

1 Friedrich Schleiermacher, *On Religion* (1799; New York, Harper, 1965), 15–16.

2 James Livingston, *Modern Christian Thought* (New York, Macmillan, 1971), 91.

3 Rowland Williams, 'Bunsen's biblical researches', in Benjamin Jowett (ed.), *Essays and Reviews* (London, Parker, 1861), 78–80.

4 Alan Stephenson, *The Rise and Decline of English Modernism* (London, SPCK, 1984), 66.

5 Ibid., 74.

6 Ibid., 73.

[7] Basil Mitchell, *The Justification of Religious Belief* (London, Macmillan 1973); Richard Swinburne, *The Existence of God* (Oxford, Clarendon Press, 1979).

[8] Interview recorded in a video *Whose World?*, ed. Adam Ford (London, CTVC, 1987).

[9] Ibid.

[10] Nicholas Lash, *Easter in Ordinary* (London, SCM, 1988), 273.

[11] John Hick, 'Religious faith as experiencing-as', in Paul Badham (ed.), *A John Hick Reader* (London, Macmillan, 1990), 37.

[12] John Hick, *Disputed Questions* (London, Macmillan, 1993), 17–32.

[13] Richard Swinburne, 'The evidential value of religious experience', in A. R. Peacocke (ed.), *The Sciences and Theology in the Twentieth Century* (Notre Dame, Ind., University of Notre Dame Press, 1981), 82–96; based on ch. 13 of his *The Existence of God* from which (p. 250) this citation is made.

[14] Ninian Smart, 'History of mysticism', in P. Edwards, *Encyclopedia of Philosophy* (New York, Macmillan and Free Press, 1967); cited in Swinburne, *The Existence of God*, 246.

[15] Caroline Franks Davis, *The Evidential Force of Religious Experience* (Oxford, Clarendon Press, 1989), 9.

[16] Ibid., 9, discussing T. R. Miles, *Religious Experience* (London, Macmillan, 1972).

[17] Badham (ed.), *A John Hick Reader*, 59.

[18] David Hay, *Religious Experience Today* (London, Mowbray, 1990), 54, 82, 83; cf. also his *Exploring Inner Space* (Harmondsworth, Penguin, 1982).

[19] Hay, *Religious Experience Today*, 57.

[20] I. Kant, *Religion within the Limits of Reason Alone* (1794; repr. New York, Harper Torchbooks, 1960), book 4, 156–63.

[21] E. Caldwell Moore, *Christian Thought since Kant* (London, Duckworth, 1912), 98.

[22] John Hick, *An Interpretation of Religion* (London, Macmillan, 1989), 12–15.

[23] Swinburne, *The Existence of God*, 273 n. 1.

[24] E. Mascall, *Words and Images* (London, Longman, 1957), 43; cf. V. Lossky, *The Mystical Theology of the Eastern Church* (London, James Clarke, 1967), 223–4.

[25] 1 Corinthians 2: 14.

[26] Swinburne, *The Existence of God*, 251.

[27] Hick, *Disputed Questions*, 26.

[28] Swinburne, *The Existence of God*, 269–70.

[29] Susan Blackmore, *Dying to Live: Science and the Near-Death Experience* (London, Grafton, 1993), 114–15.

[30] Swinburne, *The Existence of God,* 254.

[31] R. A. Moody, *Life after Life* (Atlanta, Ga, Mockingbird, 1973).

[32] Mircea Eliade, 'Mythologies of death', in F. E. Reynolds and E. H. Waugh (eds.), *Religious Encounters with Death* (Philadelphia, Pennsylvania University Press, 1977), 17.

[33] *Zohar,* vol. 2, 307; cited in M. Cox-Chapman, *Visions of Death: The Near-Death Experience* (London, Hale, 1996), 139.

[34] *Plato: The Republic* tr. H. D. P. Lee (Harmondsworth, Penguin, 1955), 11/3 (p. 394).

[35] 2 Corinthians 12: 1–5.

[36] 2 Corinthians 12: 7.

[37] St John of the Cross, *The Dark Night of the Soul,* bk. 2, ch. 24, tr. Kurt Reinhardt (London, Constable, 1957), 84.

[38] St John of the Cross, *Poems,* tr. Roy Campbell (Harmondsworth, Penguin, 1960), 51 (47–57 are all relevant).That secular love poems of that time use the phrase 'dying that I do not die' as a sexual metaphor does not prevent us from supposing that St John was using the expression in its primary sense.

[39] Karen Armstrong, *A History of God* (London, Heinemann, 1993), 163; cited by her from Jalal al-Din Suyiti, *al-itqan fi'ulum al-aq'ran* as quoted by Maxine Rodinson, *Muhammad* (London, 1971), 74.

[40] See discussion in Karen Armstrong, *Muhammad* (London, Gollancz, 1991), 138–42.

[41] Carl Becker, 'The meaning of near-death experiences' (paper presented to the Twenty-First International Conference on the Unity of the Sciences, Washington DC, 1997).

[42] Sogyal Rimpoche, *The Tibetaŋ Book of Living and Dying* (London, Routledge, 1992), 330–6.

[43] W. Y. Evans-Wentz (ed.), *The Tibetan Book of the Dead: or the After-Death Experiences on the Bardo Plane, according to Lama Kazi Dawa-Sumdup's English Rendering* (1927; 3rd edn. London, Oxford University Press, 1957), 98, 101.

[44] Ibid., 94.

[45] Bukyo Dendo Kyokai, *The Teaching of Buddha* (Tokyo, Buddhist Promoting Foundation, 1980), 218; quoting from *Amitayurdhyana-sutra.*

[46] *Daily Telegraph,* 27 Mar. 1993, magazine section, 21.

[47] Kenneth Ring, *Life at Death: A Scientific Account of the Near-Death Experience* (New York, Coward, McCann, & Geohagen, 1980), 81, 169, 240.

Notes to chapter 11: The contribution of Modernism to the contemporary understanding of world religion

[1] John Lithgow, *Modernists and Radicals* (Lampeter, MA thesis, 1983), 99–100.

[2] Henry Major, *English Modernism* (Cambridge, Mass., Harvard University Press, 1927), 213.

[3] William Temple, *Readings in St John's Gospel* (London, Macmillan, 1963), 9.

[4] I accept that there is a problem in quoting from William Temple in support of Modernism in view of the increasingly traditionalist development of his thought. However, he was a member of the MCU, and in his early life a pioneering Modernist. His ordination was the test-case as to whether a person who doubted the Virgin Birth and the bodily resurrection of Jesus could be ordained. By overruling the bishop of Oxford's refusal and ordaining Temple, Archbishop Davidson established the rights of all future Modernists. The Chalcedonian Definition proclaiming Christ as both fully God and fully human was agreed in 451 and remains the normative statement of historic orthodoxy. Yet as a young theologian Temple described the Definition as intellectually bankrupt, in his contribution to Streeter's highly controversial work *Foundations* in 1912. And, in spite of his own move back to traditionalism, he was still willing to chair the commission that wrote the *Doctrine Report* of 1938 which legitimated many key Modernist views as tenable within Anglicanism.

[5] John Hick (ed.), *The Myth of God Incarnate* (London, SCM, 1978), 181.

[6] John Hick, *An Interpretation of Religion* (London, Macmillan, 1989), 235–6.

[7] Adolf von Harnack, *What is Christianity?* (London, Benn, 1958), 110.

[8] Hastings Rashdall, *The Idea of the Atonement in Christian Theology* (London, Macmillan, 1925), 375, 411.

[9] Pope John Paul II, *Redemptor Hominis* (Rome, Encyclical Letter, 1979), para. 14.

[10] Denzinger, *The Church Teaches: Documents of the Church in English Translation* (London, Herder, 1965), 165.

[11] Rashdall, *The Idea of the Atonement in Christian Theology*, 410.

[12] Rowland Williams, *Rational Godliness* (London, Bell & Daldry, 1855), c. 19.

[13] Rowland Williams, *Parameswara-jyyana-gosthi: A Dialogue of the Knowledge of the Supreme Lord, in which are compared the claims of Christianity and Hinduism and various questions of Indian Literature fairly discussed* (Cambridge, Deighton Bell, 1856).

14 Rowland Williams, 'Bunsen's biblical researches', in B. Jowett (ed.), *Essays and Reviews* (London, Parker, 1860), 51.

15 B. H. Streeter, *The Buddha and the Christ* (London, Macmillan, 1932), 83.

16 Ibid., 86–7.

17 Ibid., 92.

18 Ibid., 110.

19 Ibid., 136.

20 John Austin Baker, *The Faith of a Christian* (London, DLT, 1996), 112.

21 Ibid., 37.

22 Qur'ān 4: 171.

23 Rowland Williams, *Rational Godliness* (Cambridge, Cambridge University Press, 1855), ch. 24.

24 St Thomas Aquinas, *Summa theologiae*, 3/94/1; cited with other similar references in Paul and Linda Badham, *Immortality or Extinction* (London, SPCK, 1984), 62.

25 St Augustine, *Confessions*, 13/36–7 (Harmondsworth, Penguin, 1961), 346.

26 *Sunday Times*, 7 Sept. 1997.

27 N. Gumbel, *Questions of Life* (London, Kingsway, 1996), 199–216.

28 The Doctrine Commission of the Church of England, *We Believe in God* (London, Church House Publishing, 1987).

29 Open Letter Group, 'An invitation to the clergy of the Church of England', 20 Sept. 1991.

30 John Hick, *Problems of Religious Pluralism* (London, Macmillan, 1985), 67ff.

Index